THE POETRY MAKERS

BOOK 3

Illustrations by John O'Connor

❧

The device at the left of the title of each
poem in this book is known as a fleuron, or
printer's flower, here used as a marker. A
different fleuron is used in each book.

THE BODLEY HEAD SERIES

The Poetry Makers

a graded anthology of poetry
for Secondary schools
chosen by

JAMES McGRATH M.A.

Deputy Headmaster
St. Pius' Secondary School
Glasgow

BOOK 3

HEINEMANN EDUCATIONAL
BOOKS LTD · LONDON

Heinemann Educational Books Ltd

LONDON EDINBURGH MELBOURNE TORONTO
SINGAPORE JOHANNESBURG AUCKLAND
HONG KONG NAIROBI IBADAN

S B N 435 14572 X

First published by The Bodley Head 1968
First published by Heinemann Educational Books Ltd
in association with The Bodley Head 1969

Published by
Heinemann Educational Books Ltd
48 Charles Street, London W1X 8AH

Printed and bound in Great Britain by
C. Tinling & Co. Ltd., Prescot

ACKNOWLEDGMENTS

We would like to thank the following for permission to reprint copyright material:

Faber & Faber Ltd. for 'O What is that Sound?' by W. H. Auden from *Collected Shorter Poems 1927-1957*; A. D. Peters & Co. Ltd. for 'Tarantella' by Hilaire Belloc from *Sonnets and Verses* (Duckworth); Gerald Duckworth Ltd. for 'Lord Hippo' by Hilaire Belloc from *Cautionary Verses*; William Heinemann Ltd. for 'Long Distance Lorry' by Philip Callow from *Turning Point*; Chatto & Windus Ltd. for 'Men in Green' by David Campbell from *Speak with the Sun*; Macmillan & Co. Ltd. for 'Ballad of the Tinker's Daughter' and 'Ballad of the Tinker's Son' by Sigerson Clifford from *Ballads of a Bogman*; Mr A. Dobson as representative of the executors of the late Austin Dobson for 'A Fancy from Fontenelle' from *The Complete Poetical Works of Dobson* (O.U.P.); J. M. Dent & Sons Ltd. for 'The Swans' by Clifford Dyment from *Axe in the Wood*; Oxford University Press for 'The Song-Maker' by Kingsley Fairbridge from *Veldt Verses*; Laurence Pollinger Ltd. for 'Out, Out—' by Robert Frost from *The Complete Poems of Robert Frost* (Cape); Punch Publications Ltd. for 'George Peters' Rock' by Crosbie Garstin; Mr Michael Gibson and Macmillan & Co. Ltd. for 'Flannan Isle' and 'The Stone' by W. W. Gibson from *Collected Poems 1905-1925*, 'The Last Shift' by W. W. Gibson from *The Golden Room and Other Poems* and 'The Ponies' by W. W. Gibson from *Fuel*; the Trustees of the Hardy Estate and Macmillan & Co. Ltd. for 'Squire Hooper' by Thomas Hardy from *The Collected Poems of Thomas Hardy*; 'Old Christmas' from *Lonesome Water* by Roy Helton. Copyright 1930 by Harper & Brothers; renewed 1958 by Roy Helton. Reprinted with the permission of Harper & Row, Publishers, Incorporated; Faber & Faber Ltd. for 'I was a Labourer' by Sean Jennett from *The Cloth of Flesh*; Mrs George Bambridge and Methuen & Co. Ltd. for 'Danny Deever' and 'Ford o' Kabul River' by Rudyard Kipling from *Barrack Room Ballads* and 'Gethsemane' by Rudyard Kipling from *The Years Between*; Houghton Mifflin Company, Boston, U.S.A. for 'Charley Lee' by Henry Herbert Knibbs from *Songs of the Lost Frontier*; Angus & Robertson Ltd. for 'Knocking Around' by Henry Lawson from

FOREWORD

A new series of poetry anthologies for secondary schools must, in an increasingly crowded field, have something particular to say for itself. THE POETRY MAKERS is the fruit of some fifteen years' experience in the teaching of poetry to boys and girls of secondary school age, and is designed as staple fare for these pupils.

The series is graded—a delicate matter, and one on which no two lovers of poetry can ever quite agree. But, again in the light of experience, I believe that users of this series will find that there is to be found in each book an overall appropriateness for the age group on which they can rely, and to which their students will respond. I have rejected arrangement by themes, a system which prejudices the student's response to the poem itself, and one which has been recently much overdone. Instead, I have juxtaposed the poems—by length, by subject matter, and by tone of voice—in the belief that such an arrangement stimulates awareness, and fosters discrimination. The order of poems within each book again reflects an idea of grading, and if the user does want poems arranged by themes he will find ample material for the class to group poems in this way *for themselves*. It will also be found that each of the first three books is in a real sense a preparation for the next. Events, moods and images which are treated at one level in, say, Book 1, will be found to recur at a new level of maturity in Book 2. The same will be found with the poets themselves, who are asked to say new things at new levels of sophistication as the series progresses.

A final word about my ultimate canon of selection: when faced with the choice, I have always preferred the concrete image to the abstract, the eventful to the static. These are books to be enjoyed, and a powerful factor to this end is that in every poem something of interest takes place.

Brief notes will be found at the end of certain poems. These are either glosses on archaisms, diction and dialect; or explanations of the poem's setting in time and place, or of its basis in history or legend.   J. McG.

7

CONTENTS

Where no author is given the poem is anonymous

A*   9

† *indicates that the text has been cut*

Long Distance Lorry

Red truck slumbering in the alley
at midday, tucked out of sight;
a wintry sun just missing the tin roof.
The driver and his mate fast asleep,
keeled over sideways, both of them,
as if sleep had hit them from one side.
Strangers. I go by surprised,
staring at them through the windscreen.
Unknowns. I go by unknown,
lingering, nobody in sight.
One is yellow about the face,
The other needs a shave.
Babes in the cab. Secrets
and journeys on their eyelids,
their faces bathed with tiredness.
I shall never see them again.

PHILIP CALLOW

❧ George Peters' Rock

'What keeps you so late, George Peters?
Black is the night with the tide-rips fuming,
Spindrift flying and breakers booming
Bull-mouthed out on the Zantam Ledges.
Haul your tackle and hoist your kedges,
Set a reef in your jib and run down
East—as the others did at sundown.
The fish are gone and the Sound's a welter
Of foam, so you'd best scud to shelter,
George Peters.'

'It's blowing strong, but I've known it stronger:
I've waited long, and I may wait longer,
Come time, come tide—but it's neither skate
That I await
Nor conger.'

'Why don't you come in, George Peters?
Hugh Town kitchens are bright and cosy,
Hugh Town windows are twinkling rosy
Over the harbour. Songs and laughter
Echo around the old inn rafter
(Tarpaulin shanties naught could muffle)
Fiddles jiggle and sea-boots shuffle
Horn-pipe measures—while in the Sound you
Crouch with the breakers moaning round you,
George Peters.'

'It couldn't be counted exactly gay here,
There's nothing but black seas breaking grey here,
But although the shore lights brightly beckon,
No less I reckon
I'll stay here.'

'Does no one wait you, George Peters?
Is there no girl in all St. Mary's
Quickens your fancy? Surely there is
Some dark head you have watched in chapel,
Some cheek pink as the flower of apple,
Curved deliciously, dimple-dented,
To wake your blood when the lily-scented,
Soft, sea-murmurous dusk is stealing
Spangled with stars and sea-lights wheeling,
George Peters?'

'It's a pale woman I keep tryst with,
She slips quietly out of the mist with
Never a sound but the water drips,
And it's cold, cold lips
I'm kissed with.
Her foam-white arms go over and round me,
And her green hair binds me as it bound me
On that first night she rose from the deep,
Lulled me to sleep
And drowned me.'

CROSBIE GARSTIN

kedges: anchors
The place-names in this poem are to be found in the Scilly Isles.

13

✂ Birds' Nests

The summer nests uncovered by autumn wind,
Some torn, others dislodged, all dark,
Everyone sees them: low or high in tree,
Or hedge, or single bush, they hang like a mark.

Since there's no need of eyes to see them with
I cannot help a little shame
That I missed most, even at eye's level, till
The leaves blew off and made the seeing no game.

'Tis a light pang. I like to see the nests
Still in their places, now first known,
At home and by far roads. Boys knew them not,
Whatever jays and squirrels may have done.

And most I like the winter nests deep-hid
That leaves and berries fell into:
Once a dormouse dined there on hazel-nuts,
And grass and goose-grass seeds found soil and grew.

EDWARD THOMAS

14

❧ Ford o' Kabul River

Kabul town's by Kabul river—
Blow the trumpet, draw the sword—
There I lef' my mate for ever,
Wet an' drippin' by the ford.
Ford, ford, ford o' Kabul river,
Ford o' Kabul river in the dark!
There's the river up an' brimmin', an' there's 'arf a squadron swimmin'
'Cross the ford o' Kabul river in the dark.

Kabul town's a blasted place—
Blow the trumpet, draw the sword—
'Strewth, I shan't forget 'is face
Wet an' drippin' by the ford!
Ford, ford, ford o' Kabul river,
Ford o' Kabul river in the dark!
Keep the crossing-stakes beside you, an' they will surely guide you
'Cross the ford o' Kabul river in the dark.

Kabul town is sun an' dust—
Blow the trumpet, draw the sword—
I'd ha' sooner drownded fust
'Stead of 'im beside the ford.
Ford, ford, ford o' Kabul river,
Ford o' Kabul river in the dark!
You can 'ear the 'orses threshin'; you can 'ear the men a-splashin',
'Cross the ford o' Kabul river in the dark.

Kabul town was ours to take—
Blow the trumpet, draw the sword—
I'd ha' left it for 'is sake—
'Im that left me by the ford.

Ford, ford, ford o' Kabul river,
Ford o' Kabul river in the dark!
It's none so bloomin' dry there; ain't you never comin' nigh
   there,
'Cross the ford o' Kabul river in the dark?

Kabul town'll go to hell—
Blow the trumpet, draw the sword—
'Fore I see 'im 'live an' well—
'Im the best beside the ford.
Ford, ford, ford o' Kabul river,
Ford o' Kabul river in the dark!
Gawd 'elp 'em if they blunder, for their boots'll pull 'em
   under,
By the ford o' Kabul river in the dark.

Turn your 'orse from Kabul town—
Blow the bugle, draw the sword—
'Im an' 'arf my troop is down,
Down and drownded by the ford.
Ford, ford, ford o' Kabul river,
Ford o' Kabul river in the dark!
There's the river low an' fallin', but it ain't no use a-callin'
'Cross the ford o' Kabul river in the dark!

RUDYARD KIPLING

This poem describes an incident of the Second Afghan War (1878-
1880) when a squadron of the 10th Hussars, crossing the river in
early morning mist, mistook the fording place and entered at deep
water. Many were swept away.

♫ The Ballad of the Tinker's Son

I was in school, 'twas the first of May,
The day the tinker came
With his wild wide eyes like a frightened hare's,
And his head with its thatch on flame.

We liked the length of his bare brown legs,
The patches upon his clothes,
The grimy strength of his unwashed hands
And the freckles about his nose.

The master polished his rimless specs
And he stared at him hard and long,
Then he stood him up on a shaky bench
And called on him for a song.

The tinker boy looked at our laughing lips,
Then with voice like a timid bird's
He followed the master's bidding
And these are his singing words.

'My father was jailed for sheep-stealing,
My mother is black as a witch,
My sister off-ran with the Sheridan clan,
And my brother's dead-drunk in a ditch.

'O Tralee jail would kill the devil,
But Tralee jail won't kill my da,
I'll mend ye a kettle for one-and-fourpence
And bring home porter to my ma.'

He bowed his head as the schoolhouse shook
With the cheers of everyone,

Then the master made me share my desk
With the raggedy tinker's son.

The days dragged by and he sat down there,
His brown eyes still afraid,
He heard the scholars' drowsy hum
And, turning to me, he said . . .

'Now what would I want with x and y
And I singing the crooked towns,
Or showing a drunken farmer
The making of silver crowns?

'And will Euclid teach me to light a fire
Of green twigs in the rain,
Or how to twist a pheasant's neck
So it will not shout with pain?

'And what would I want with ancient verse
Or the meaning of Latin words
When all the poetry I'll ever need
Rings the throats of the singing birds?'

But he stayed at school and his flowering mind
Grew quick as a swooping hawk;
Then came a day when we said goodbye
To the master who smelt of chalk.

He went to the life of the ribbon roads
And the lore of the tinker bands;
They chained my bones to an office stool
And my soul to a clock's cold hands.

But I often thought of my tinker friend
And I cursed the smirking luck

That didn't make me a tinker man
Fighting the road to Puck.

With a red-haired wife and a piebald horse,
And a splendid caravan,
Roving the roads with Cartys and Wards,
The O'Briens or the Coffey clan.

The years went by and the Trouble came,
And I found myself again
Back where I whittled the worn desks,
With the mountains and the rain.

They put a trench-coat on my back,
And in my hands a gun,
And up in the hills with the fighting men
I found the tinker's son.

And there on the slopes of the Kerry hills
Our love grew still more strong,
And we watched the wrens on the yellow whins
Spill their thimblefuls of song.

There came a truce and I shook his hand
For a while our fighting done;
But I never spoke a word again
To the red-haired tinker's son. . . .

'Tis many a year since he went away
And over the roads the vans
Wheel gaily to horse and cattle fairs
With the O'Brien and the Coffey clans.

The tinker's son should be back again
With the roads and the life he knew,
But I put a bullet through his brain
In nineteen twenty-two.

SIGERSON CLIFFORD

Puck: the Tinkers' Fair.

The Trouble, or Troubles, were the hostilities between the Irish Republican Army, demanding Home Rule for Ireland, and the British Government (1921). In December 1921, a treaty was signed dividing Ireland into the Irish Free State and Northern Ireland, which remained part of the British Crown.

In 1922, Civil War broke out between those Irishmen who accepted the Treaty and those who did not.

❧ Mother Wept

Mother wept, and father sigh'd;
With delight aglow
Cried the lad, 'To-morrow,' cried,
'To the pit I go.'

Up and down the place he sped,—
Greeted old and young;
Far and wide the tidings spread;
Clapt his hands and sung.

Came his cronies; some to gaze
Wrapp'd in wonder; some
Free with counsel; some with praise;
Some with envy dumb.

'May he,' many a gossip cried,
'Be from peril kept.'
Father hid his face and sigh'd,
Mother turn'd and wept.

JOSEPH SKIPSEY

﹩ The Station Master of Lone Prairie

An empty bench, a sky of greyest etching,
    A bare, bleak shed in blackest silhouette,
Twelve yards of platform, and beyond them stretching
    Twelve miles of prairie glimmering through the wet.

North, South, East, West—the same dull grey persistence,
    The tattered vapours of a vanished train,
The narrowing rails that meet to pierce the distance,—
    Or break the columns of the far-off rain.

Naught but myself—nor form nor figure breaking
    The long hushed level and stark shining waste—
Nothing that moves to fill the vision aching,
    When the last shadow fled in sullen haste.

Nothing but this. Ah, yes! beside the station
    Its stiff gaunt keeper turns to me at last,
Beckoning me with a wooden salutation—
    Raised like his signal—when the up-train passed.

Offering the bench, beside him, with dumb gesture—
    Born of the reticence in sky and air—
Then sat we both—enwrapped in that one vesture—
    Of silence, sadness, and unspoken care.

Each following his own thought—around us darkening
    The rain-washed boundaries and stretching track—
Each following those dim parallels, and hearkening
    For long-lost voices that would not come back.

Until unasked—I knew not why or wherefore—
    He yielded, bit by bit, his dreary past,
Like gathered clouds that seemed to thicken there for
    Some dull down-dropping of their care at last.

Long had he lived there. When a boy, had started
  From the stacked corn the Indian's painted face;
Heard the wolves howl the wearying waste that parted
  His father's hut from the last camping place.

Nature had mocked him; thrice had claimed the reaping
  With scythes of fire the land she once had sown;
Sent the tornado—round his hearthstone heaping
  Rafters, dead faces—that were like his own.

Then came the War Time. When its shadow beckoned
  He had walked dumbly where the flag had led
Through swamp and fen—unknown, unpraised, un-
    reckoned,
  To famine, fever, and a prison-bed.

Till the storm passed, and the slow time returning
  Cast him, a wreck, beneath his native sky.
Here near his home, gave him the chance of earning
  Scant means to live—who won the right to die.

All this I heard, or seemed to hear, half bending
  With the low murmur of the coming breeze,
The call of some lost bird, and the unending
  And tireless sobbing of those grassy seas.

Until at length the spell of desolation
  Broke with a trembling star and far-off cry.
The coming train! I glanced around the station.
  All was as empty as the upper sky.

Naught but myself—nor form nor figure waking
  The long hushed level and stark shining waste—
Naught but myself, that cry, and the dull shaking
  Of wheel and axle, stopped in breathless haste!

23

'Now then—look sharp! Eh, what? The Station-Master?
Thar's none! We stopped here of our own accord.
The man got killed in that down-train disaster
   This time last evening. Right there! All aboard!'

BRET HARTE

❧ Coroner's Jury

He was the doctor up to Coombe,
Quiet-spoke, dark, weared a moustache,
And one night his wife's mother died
After her meal, and he was tried
      For poisoning her.

Evidence come up dark 's a bag,
But onions is like arsenic:
'Twas eating they, his lawyer said,
And rabbit, 'fore she went to bed
      That took her off.

Jury withdrew. 'He saved my child,'
Says 'Lias Lee. 'Think to his wife,'
Says one. 'I tell 'ee, a nit's life
That there old 'ooman led 'em both—
      Tedious old toad.'

'Give en six months,' says easy Joe.
'You can't do that, sirs,' foreman said,
' 'Tis neck or nothing, yes or no.'
'All right then, sir,' says Joe. ' 'Tis no,
      Not guilty, sir.'

'You, Jabez Halls ?' 'I brings it in
Rabbit and onions; that's my thought.
If that didn't kill her, sirs, it ought,
To her age.' So us brought it in
      Rabbit and onions.

Doctor went free, but missis died
Soon afterward, she broke her heart.
Still Doctor bide on twenty year
Walking the moors, keeping apart
        And quiet, like.

L. A. G. STRONG

✺ At the Cedars

You had two girls, Baptiste,
One is Virginie—
Hold hard, Baptiste!
Listen to me.

The whole drive was jammed
In that bend at the Cedars,
The rapids were dammed
With the logs tight rammed
And crammed; you might know
The Devil had clinched them below.

We worked three days—not a budge,
'She's as tight as a wedge,
On the ledge,'
Says our foreman;
'Mon Dieu! boys, look here,
We must get this thing clear.'
He cursed at the men
And we went for it then;
With our cant-dogs arow
We just gave he-yo-ho
When she gave a big shove
From above.

The gang yelled and tore
For the shore,
The logs gave a grind
Like a wolf's jaws behind,
And as quick as a flash,
With a shove and a crash,
They were down in a mash,
But I and ten more,
All but Isaac Dufour
Were ashore.

He leaped on a log in front of the rush,
And shot out from the bind
While the jam roared behind;
As he floated along
He balanced his pole
And tossed us a song.
But just as we cheered,
Up darted a log from the bottom,
Leaped thirty feet square and fair,
And came down on his own.

He went up like a block
With the shock,
And when he was there
In the air,
Kissed his hand
To the land;
When he dropped
My heart stopped,
For the front logs had caught him
And crushed him;
When he rose in his place
There was blood on his face.

There were some girls, Baptiste,
Picking berries on the hillside,
Where the river curls, Baptiste,
You know—on the still side;
One was down by the water;
She saw Isaac
Fall back.

She did not scream, Baptiste,
She launched her canoe;
It did seem, Baptiste,
That she wanted to die too,

For before you could think
The birch cracked like a shell
In that rush of hell
And I saw them both sink—

Baptiste!—
He had two girls,
One is Virginie;
What God calls the other
Is not known to me.

DUNCAN CAMPBELL SCOTT

cant-dogs: hooked handspikes

A Narrow Fellow in the Grass

A narrow fellow in the grass
Occasionally rides;
You may have met him,—did you not?
His notice sudden is.

The grass divides as with a comb,
A spotted shaft is seen;
And then it closes at your feet
And opens further on.

He likes a boggy acre,
A floor too cool for corn.
Yet when a child, and barefoot,
I more than once, at morn,

Have passed, I thought, a whip-lash
Upbraiding in the sun,—
When, stooping to secure it,
It wrinkled, and was gone.

Several of nature's people
I know, and they know me;
I feel for them a transport
Of cordiality;

But never met this fellow,
Attended or alone,
Without a tighter breathing,
And zero at the bone.

EMILY DICKINSON

❧ Carentan O Carentan

Trees in the old days used to stand
And shape a shady lane
Where lovers wandered hand in hand
Who came from Carentan.

This was the shining green canal
Where we came two by two
Walking at combat-interval.
Such trees we never knew.

The day was early June, the ground
Was soft and bright with dew.
Far away the guns did sound,
But here the sky was blue.

The sky was blue, but there a smoke
Hung still above the sea
Where the ships together spoke
To towns we could not see.

Could you have seen us through a glass
You would have said a walk
Of farmers out to turn the grass,
Each with his own hay-fork.

The watchers in their leopard suits
Waited till it was time,
And aimed between the belt and boot
And let the barrel climb.

I must lie down at once, there is
A hammer at my knee.
And call it death or cowardice,
Don't count again on me.

Everything's all right, Mother,
Everyone gets the same
At one time or another.
It's all in the game.

I never strolled, nor ever shall,
Down such a leafy lane.
I never drank in a canal,
Nor ever shall again.

There is a whistling in the leaves
And it is not the wind,
The twigs are falling from the knives
That cut men to the ground.

Tell me, Master-Sergeant,
The way to turn and shoot.
But the Sergeant's silent
That taught me how to do it.

O Captain, show us quickly
Our place upon the map.
But the Captain's sickly
And taking a long nap.

Lieutenant, what's my duty,
My place in the platoon?
He too's a sleeping beauty,
Charmed by that strange tune.

Carentan O Carentan
Before we met with you
We never yet had lost a man
Or known what death could do.

LOUIS SIMPSON

Carentan is a village in Normandy. During the early days of the invasion of 1944 the 101st American Airborne Division were given orders to capture it. Louis Simpson took part in the engagement which was the first battle experience of the company in which he served. Heavy casualties were inflicted on the brave but inexperienced troops by German parachute infantry in 'leopard suits',—a mixture of mustard brown and yellow for camouflage—hidden in trees.

A Fancy from Fontenelle

The Rose in the garden slipped her bud,
And she laughed in the pride of her youthful blood
As she thought of the Gardener standing by—
'He is old—so old! And he soon must die!'

The full Rose waxed in the warm June air,
And she spread and spread till her heart lay bare;
And she laughed once more as she heard his tread—
'He is older now! He will soon be dead!'

But the breeze of the morning blew, and found
That the leaves of the blown Rose strewed the ground;
And he came at noon, that Gardener old,
And he raked them gently under the mould.

And I wove the thing to a random rhyme,
For the Rose is Beauty, the Gardener, Time.

AUSTIN DOBSON

❧ Helen of Kirkconnell

I wish I were where Helen lies,
Night and day on me she cries:
O that I were where Helen lies,
On fair Kirkconnell lea!

Curst be the heart that thought the thought,
And curst the hand that fired the shot,
When in my arms burd Helen dropt,
And died to succour me!

O think na ye my heart was sair,
When my Love dropt and spak nae mair!
There did she swoon wi' meikle care,
On fair Kirkconnell lea.

As I went down the waterside,
None but my foe to be my guide,
None but my foe to be my guide,
On fair Kirkconnell lea;

I lighted down, my sword to draw,
I hacked him in pieces sma',
I hacked him in pieces sma',
For her sake that died for me.

O Helen fair, beyond compare!
I'll mak a garland o' thy hair,
Shall bind my heart for evermair,
Until the day I die!

O that I were where Helen lies!
Night and day on me she cries;
Out of my bed she bids me rise,
Says, 'Haste, and come to me!'

O Helen fair! O Helen chaste!
If I were with thee, I'd be blest,
Where thou lies low, and taks thy rest
On fair Kirkconnell lea.

I wish my grave were growing green,
A winding-sheet drawn o'er my een,
And I in Helen's arms lying
On fair Kirkconnell lea.

I wish I were where Helen lies!
Night and day on me she cries:
And I am weary of the skies
For her sake that died for me.

ANON.

burd: young woman

The young woman here was Helen Irving, daughter of the laird of Kirkconnell. She had two suitors, Adam Fleming, and a young man named Bell whom her family preferred. Helen and Adam Fleming had to meet secretly until one day they were seen by Bell near the River Kirtle. The events described in the ballad then followed. Adam Fleming was later buried in the same grave as Helen in Kirkconnell churchyard.

37

❧ The Snowslide

It came so slow.
I remember, we sweated and cursed across the bulge
of the white snow sloping; our tongues dry and our shirts
clung on our legs; loads bit at our back
till we sat down.
Then, from above, the murmur of little men,
rustle and click and roll of a loosened line
as they came flickering, flocking out from the jaws
where the gully held them, gently curious down.
Just a line of snowballs, as on a Christmas lawn
a child quarries and rolls, then rolling along
makes bigger and bigger; but lawns do not tilt and turn
over, then down.
You were below, when the loping invaders came
high as my arm, but the ice-axe held and they passed
disappointed to you, you rock in the swell of seas,
too tough for this wash ever to break your hold,
they came so slow.
But they came and came, and their gathering overbore
gently and slow, gently they carried you down
like a king reclining—look!—where the whaleback bow
heels into blue nothing, and leagues beyond
suddenly the valley's green edges the snow.
Then there was silence, hiss of the slide soft hushed.
The mountains lay, stood, reared like creatures that dream,
lovely in the sunlight: ebony, silver and silk,
just as before. But I loathed them, trembling and sick.
You were gone.

WILFRED NOYCE

The Bunyip and the Whistling Kettle

I knew a most superior camper
  Whose methods were absurdly wrong,
He did not live on tea and damper
  But took a little stove along.

And every place he came to settle
  He spread with gadgets saving toil,
He even had a whistling kettle
  To warn him it was on the boil.

Beneath the waratahs and wattles,
  Boronia and coolibah,
He scattered paper, cans and bottles,
  And parked his nasty little car.

He camped, this sacrilegious stranger
  (The moon was at the full that week)
Once in a spot that teemed with danger
  Beside a bunyip-haunted creek.

He spread his junk but did not plunder,
  Hoping to stay the weekend long;
He watched the bloodshot sun go under
  Across the silent billabong.

He ate canned food without demurring,
  He put the kettle on for tea.
He did not see the water stirring
  Far out beside a sunken tree.

Then, for the day had made him swelter
  And night was hot and tense to spring,
He donned a bathing-suit in shelter
  And left the firelight's friendly ring.

He felt the water kiss and tingle.
  He heard the silence—none too soon!
A ripple broke against the shingle,
  And dark with blood it met the moon.

Abandoned in the hush, the kettle
  Screamed as it guessed its master's plight,
And loud it screamed, the lifeless metal,
  Far into the malicious night.

JOHN MANIFOLD

bunyip: man-eating swamp monster in Australian legend
damper: bread baked in a pan
 waratahs, wattles, boronia, coolibah: Australian shrubs
billabong: creek

❧ Knocking Around

Weary old wife, with the bucket and cow,
'How's your son Jack? and where is he now?'
Haggard old eyes that turn to the west—
'Boys will be boys, and he's gone with the rest!'
Grief without tears and grief without sound;
'Somewhere up-country he's knocking around.'
   Knocking around with a vagabond crew,
   Does for himself what a mother would do;
   May be in trouble and may be hard up.
   May be in want of a bite or a sup.
   Dead of the fever, or lost in the drought,
   Lonely old Mother! he's knocking about.
Wiry old man at the tail of the plough,
'Heard of Jack lately? and where is he now?'
Pauses a moment his forehead to wipe,
Drops the rope reins while he feels for his pipe,
Scratches his grey head in sorrow or doubt;
'Somewhere or other he's knocking about.'
   Knocking about on the runs of the West,
   Holding his own with the worst and the best,
   Breaking in horses and risking his neck,
   Droving or shearing and making a cheque;
   Straight as sapling—six foot and sound,
   Jack's all right when he's knocking around.

HENRY LAWSON

cheque: check

✧ Ballad of the Goodly Fere

Simon Zelotes Speaketh It Somewhile After The Crucifixion

Ha' we lost the goodliest fere o' all
For the priests and the gallows tree?
Aye lover he was of brawny men,
O' ships and the open sea.

When they came wi' a host to take Our Man
His smile was good to see,
'First let these go!' quo' our Goodly Fere,
'Or I'll see ye damned,' says he.

Aye he sent us out through the crossed high spears
And the scorn of his laugh rang free,
'Why took ye not me when I walked about
Alone in the town?' says he.

Oh we drunk his 'Hale' in the good red wine
When we last made company,
No capon priest was the Goodly Fere
But a man o' men was he.

I ha' seen him drive a hundred men
Wi' a bundle o' cords swung free,
That they took the high and holy house
For their pawn and treasury.

They'll no' get him a' in a book I think
Though they write it cunningly;
No mouse of the scrolls was the Goodly Fere
But aye loved the open sea.

If they think they ha' snared our Goodly Fere
They are fools to the last degree.

'I'll go to the feast,' quo' our Goodly Fere,
'Though I go to the gallows tree.'

'Ye ha' seen me heal the lame and blind,
And wake the dead,' says he,
'Ye shall see one thing to master all:
'Tis how a brave man dies on the tree.'

A son of God was the Goodly Fere
That bade us his brothers be.
I ha' seen him cow a thousand men.
I ha' seen him upon the tree.

He cried no cry when they drave the nails
And the blood gushed hot and free,
The hounds of the crimson sky gave tongue
But never a cry cried he.

I ha' seen him cow a thousand men
On the hills o' Galilee,
They whined as he walked out calm between
Wi' his eyes like the grey o' the sea.

Like the sea that brooks no voyaging
With the winds unleashed and free,
Like the sea that he cowed at Genseret
Wi' twey words spoke suddently.

A master of men was the Goodly Fere,
A mate of the wind and sea,
If they think they ha' slain our Goodly Fere
They are fools eternally.

I ha' seen him eat o' the honey-comb
Sin' they nailed him to the tree.

EZRA POUND

Fere: mate, companion
Simon Zelotes: Simon the Zealous

Gethsemane

1914-18

The Garden called Gethsemane
In Picardy it was,
And there the people came to see
The English soldiers pass.
We used to pass—we used to pass
Or halt, as it might be,
And ship our masks in case of gas
Beyond Gethsemane.

The Garden called Gethsemane,
It held a pretty lass,
But all the time she talked to me
I prayed my cup might pass.
The officer sat on the chair,
The men lay on the grass,
And all the time we halted there
I prayed my cup might pass.

It didn't pass—it didn't pass—
It didn't pass from me.
I drank it when we met the gas
Beyond Gethsemane.

RUDYARD KIPLING

44

❧ I Know Some Lonely
Houses off the Road

I know some lonely houses off the road
A robber'd like the look of,—
Wooden barred,
And windows hanging low,
Inviting to
A portico,

Where two could creep:
One hand the tools,
The other peep
To make sure all's asleep.
Old-fashioned eyes,
Not easy to surprise!

How orderly the kitchen'd look by night,
With just a clock,—
But they could gag the tick,
And mice won't bark;
And so the walls don't tell,
None will.

A pair of spectacles ajar just stir—
An almanac's aware.
Was it the mat winked,
Or a nervous star?
The moon slides down the stair
To see who's there.

There's plunder,—where?
Tankard, or spoon,
Earring, or stone,
A watch, some ancient brooch
To match the grandmamma,
Staid sleeping there.

Day rattles, too;
Stealth's slow;
The sun has got as far
As the third sycamore.
Screams chanticleer,
'Who's there?'

And echoes, trains away,
Sneer—'Where?'
While the old couple, just astir,
Think that the sunrise left the door ajar!

EMILY DICKINSON

✣ Peggy Said Good Morning

Peggy said good morning and I said good-bye,
When farmers dib the corn and laddies sow the rye.
Young Peggy's face was commonsense and I was rather shy
When I met her in the morning when the farmers sow the
    rye.

Her half-laced boots fit tightly as she tripped along the
    grass,
And she set her foot so lightly where the early bee doth pass.
Oh, Peggy was a young thing, her face was commonsense,
I courted her about the spring and loved her ever thence.

Oh, Peggy was a young thing and bonny as to size;
Her lips were cherries of the spring and hazel were her eyes.
Oh, Peggy, she was straight and tall as is the poplar-tree,
Smooth as the freestone of the wall, and very dear to me.

Oh, Peggy's gown was chocolate and full of cherries white:
I keep a bit on't for her sake and love her day and night.
I drest myself just like a prince and Peggy went to woo,
But she's been gone some ten years since, and I know not
    what to do.

JOHN CLARE

❧ First Fight

Tonight, then, is the night;
Stretched on the massage table,
Wrapped in his robe, he breathes
Liniment and sweat
And tries to close his ears
To the roaring of the crowd,
A mirky sea of noise
That bears upon its tide
The frail sound of the bell
And brings the cunning fear
That he might not do well,
Not fear of bodily pain
But that his tight-lipped pride
Might be sent crashing down,
His white ambition slain,
Knocked spinning the glittering crown.
How could his spirit bear
That ignominious fall?
Not hero but a clown
Spurned or scorned by all.
The thought appals, and he
Feels sudden envy for
The roaring crowd outside
And wishes he were there,
Anonymous and safe,
Calm in the tolerant air,
Would almost choose to be
Anywhere but here.

II

The door blares open suddenly,
The room is sluiced with row;
His second says, 'We're on next fight,

48

We'd better get going now.
You got your gumshield, haven't you?
Just loosen up—that's right—
Don't worry, Boy, you'll be okay
Once you start to fight.'

Out of the dressing room, along
The neutral passage to
The yelling cavern where the ring
Through the haze of blue
Tobacco smoke is whitewashed by
The aching glare of light:
Geometric ropes are stretched as taut
As this boy's nerves are tight.

And now he's in his corner where
He tries to look at ease;
He feels the crowd's sharp eyes as they
Prick and pry and tease;
He hears them murmur like the sea
Or some great dynamo:
They are not hostile yet they wish
To see his lifeblood flow.
His adversary enters now;
The Boy risks one quick glance;
He does not see an enemy
But something there by chance,
Not human even, but a cold
Abstraction to defeat,
A problem to be solved by guile,
Quick hands and knowing feet.
The fighters' names are shouted out;
They leave their corners for
The touch of gloves and brief commands;
The disciplines of war.
Back in their corners, stripped of robes,

49

They hear the bell clang *one*
Brazen syllable which says
The battle has begun.

III

Bite on gumshield,
Guard held high,
The crowd are silenced,
All sounds die.
Lead with the left,
Again, again;
Watch for the opening,
Feint and then
Hook to the body
But he's blocked it and
Slammed you back
With a fierce right hand.
Hang on grimly,
The fog will clear,
Sweat in your nostrils,
Grease and fear.
You're hurt and staggering,
Shocked to know
That the story's altered:
He's the hero!

But the mist is clearing,
The referee snaps
A rapid warning
And he smartly taps
Your hugging elbow
And then you step back
Ready to counter
The next attack.
But the first round finishes

Without mishap.
You suck in the air
From the towel's skilled flap.
A voice speaks urgently
Close to your ear:
'Keep your left going, Boy,
Stop him getting near.
He wants to get close to you,
So jab him off hard;
When he tries to slip below,
Never mind your guard,
Crack him with a solid right,
Hit him on the chin,
A couple downstairs
And then he'll pack it in.'

Slip in the gumshield
Bite on it hard,
Keep him off with your left,
Never drop your guard.
Try a left hook,
But he crosses with a right
Smack on your jaw
And Guy Fawkes' Night
Flashes and dazzles
Inside your skull,
Your knees go bandy
And you almost fall.
Keep the left jabbing,
Move around the ring,
Don't let him catch you with
Another hook or swing.
Keep your left working,
Keep it up high,
Stab it out straight and hard,
Again—above the eye.

Sweat in the nostrils,
But nothing now of fear,
You're moving smooth and confident
In comfortable gear.
Jab with the left again,
Quickly move away;
Feint and stab another in,
See him duck and sway.
Now for the pay-off punch,
Smash it hard inside;
It thuds against his jaw, he falls,
Limbs spread wide.
And suddenly you hear the roar,
Hoarse music of the crowd,
Voicing your hot ecstasy,
Triumphant, male and proud.

IV

Now in the sleepless darkness of his room
The Boy, in bed, remembers. Suddenly
The victory tastes sour. The man he fought
Was not a thing, as lifeless as a broom,
He was a man who hoped and trembled too;
What of him now? What was *he* going through?
And then The Boy bites hard on resolution:
Fighters can't pack pity with their gear,
And yet a bitter taste stays with the notion;
He's forced to swallow down one treacherous tear.
But that's the last. He is a boy no longer;
He is a man, a fighter, such as jeer
At those who make salt beads with melting eyes,
Whatever might cry out, is hurt, or dies.

VERNON SCANNELL

❧ Farmer's Daughter

Queen Mary, Queen Mary, my age is sixteen,
My father's a farmer on yonder green.
He's plenty of money to dress me, an' a',
An' there's *nae* bonnie laddie will tak' me awa'!

This morning I rose and I looked in the glass;
Says I to myself: 'What a handsome young lass!'
I tossed up my head and I gave a "Ha! ha!"
There's nae bonnie laddie will tak' *me* awa'!

ANON.

53

✄ The Twa Brothers

There were twa brothers at the school,
And when they got awa'—
It's 'Will ye play at the stane-chucking,
Or will ye play at ba',
Or will ye gae up to yon hill head?
And there we'll warsell a fa'.'—

'I winna play at the stane-chucking,
Nor will I play at ba',
But I'll gae up to yon bonnie green hill,
And there we'll warsell a fa'.'

They warsled up, they warsled down,
Till John fell to the ground;
A dirk fell out of William's pouch
And gave John a deadly wound.

'O lift me upon your back,
Tak me to yon well fair,
And wash my bluidy wounds o'er and o'er,
And they'll ne'er bleed nae mair.'

He's lifted his brother upon his back,
Ta'en him to yon well fair;
He's washed his bluidy wounds o'er and o'er,
But they bleed aye mair and mair.

'Tak' aff, tak' aff my holland sark,
And rive it gair by gair,
And row it in my bluidy wounds,
And they'll ne'er bleed nae mair.'

He's taken aff his holland sark
And torn it gair by gair;
He's rowed it in his bluidy wounds,
But they bleed aye mair and mair.

'O tak' now aff my green cleiding,
And row me saftly in;
And carry me up yon kirk style,
Where the grass grows fair and green.'

He's taken aff the green cleiding,
And rowed him saftly in;
He's laid him down by yon kirk style,
Where the grass grows fair and green.

'What will ye say to your father dear,
When ye gae home at e'en?'
'I'll say ye're lying at yon kirk style,
Where the grass grows fair and green.'—

'O no, O no, my brother dear,
O you must not say so;
But say I'm gone to a foreign land,
Where nae man does me know.'

When he sat in his father's chair,
He grew baith pale and wan.
'O what blude's that upon your brow?
And where is your brother John?'—

'It is the blude o' my gude grey steed—
He wouldna ride wi' me.'—
'O thy steed's blude was ne'er sae red,
Nor ne'er sae dear to me!—

'O what blude's that upon your cheek?
O dear son, tell to me.'—
'It is the blude of my greyhound,
He wouldna hunt for me.'—

'O thy hound's blude was ne'er sae red,
Nor ne'er sae dear to me;
O what blude's this upon your hand?
O dear son tell to me.'

'It is the blude of my gay goshawk,
He wadna flee for me.'—
'O thy hawk's blude was ne'er sae red,
Nor ne'er sae dear to me;

'O what blude's this upon your dirk?
Dear Willie, tell to me.'—
'It is the blude of my ae brother,
And dule and wae is me!'

'O what sall I say to your mither?
Dear Willie tell to me.'—
'I'll saddle my steed and awa' I'll ride
To dwell in some far country.'—

'O when will ye come hame again?
Dear Willie, tell to me.'—
'When the sun and moon dance on yon green;
And that will never be!'

ANON.

warsell a fa': wrestle a fall
holland sark: linen shirt
rive it gair by gair: tear it into strips
row (p. 54): dab
cleiding: clothing
row (p. 55): wrap
dule: grief

56

Danny Deever

'What are the bugles blowin' for ?' said Files-on-Parade.
'To turn you out, to turn you out,' the Colour-Sergeant said.
'What makes you look so white, so white ?' said Files-on-Parade.
'I'm dreadin' what I've got to watch,' the Colour-Sergeant said.
For they're hangin' Danny Deever, you can hear the Dead March play,
The regiment's in 'ollow square—they're hangin' him to-day;
They've taken of his buttons off an' cut his stripes away,
An' they're hangin' Danny Deever in the mornin'.

'What makes the rear-rank breathe so 'ard ?' said Files-on-Parade.
'It's bitter cold, it's bitter cold,' the Colour-Sergeant said.
'What makes that front-rank man fall down ?' said Files-on-Parade.
'A touch o' sun, a touch o' sun,' the Colour-Sergeant said.
They are hangin' Danny Deever, they are marchin' of 'im round,
They 'ave 'alted Danny Deever by 'is coffin on the ground;
An' 'e'll swing in 'arf a minute for a sneakin' shootin' hound—
O they're hangin' Danny Deever in the mornin'!

' 'Is cot was right-'and cot to mine,' said Files-on-Parade.
' 'E's sleepin' out an' far tonight,' the Colour-Sergeant said.
'I've drunk 'is beer a score o' times,' said Files-on-Parade.
' 'E's drinkin' bitter beer alone,' the Colour-Sergeant said.
They're hangin' Danny Deever, you must mark 'im to 'is place,

For 'e shot a comrade sleepin'—you must look 'im in the
    face;
Nine 'undred of 'is county an' the Regiment's disgrace,
While they're hangin' Danny Deever in the mornin'.

'What's that so black agin the sun?' said Files-on-Parade.
'It's Danny fightin' 'ard for life,' the Colour-Sergeant said.
'What's that that whimpers over'ead?' said Files-on-
    Parade.
'It's Danny's soul that's passin' now,' the Colour-Sergeant
    said.
For they're done with Danny Deever, you can 'ear the
    quickstep play,
The Regiment's in column, an' they're marchin' us away;
Ho! the young recruit's are shakin', and they'll want their
    beer today
After hangin' Danny Deever in the mornin'!

RUDYARD KIPLING

58

❧ Lord Hippo

Lord Hippo suffered fearful loss
By putting money on a horse
Which he believed, if it were pressed,
Would run far faster than the rest:
For someone who was in the know
Had confidently told him so.
But on the morning of the race
It only took the *seventh* place!
Picture the Viscount's great surprise!
He scarcely could believe his eyes!
He sought the Individual who
Had laid him odds at 9 to 2,
Suggesting as a useful tip
That they should enter Partnership
And put to joint account the debt
Arising from his foolish bet.
But when the Bookie—oh! my word,
I only wish you could have heard
The way he roared he did not think,
And hoped that they might strike him pink!
Lord Hippo simply turned and ran
From this infuriated man.
Despairing, maddened, and distraught
He utterly collapsed and sought
His Sire, the Earl of Potamus,
And brokenly addressed him thus:
'Dread Sire—to-day—at Ascot—I . . .'
His genial parent made reply:
'Come! Come! Come! Come! don't look so glum!
Trust your Papa and name the sum . . .
. . . Fifteen hundred thousand? . . . Hum!
However . . . stiffen up, you wreck;
Boys will be boys—so here's the cheque!'

Lord Hippo, feeling deeply—well,
More grateful than he dared to tell—
Punted the lot on Little Nell:—
And got a telegram at dinner
To say that he had backed the winner!

HILAIRE BELLOC

✥ Man With Scythe

Shambling Frank the labourer
Lacking all grace,
With less than a gorilla's comeliness
Of gait or face,

With his loose mouth that bares
Almost to the roots
Files of skewbald fangs
Ragged as recruits,

With hideous hurricane-bawl
Close to one's ear,
And sidelong watery
Frogspawn leer,

See him transfigured:
Half a meadow away
Frank with his scythe marches
Against the hay.

That great mandible, sweeping
Its underslung arc,
Munching a field flat
Between morning and dark,

Sways him into dignity.
The stiff wide stance
Easy roundabout swing
And deliberate advance,

The occasional pause erect
For clash and chime
Of whetstone on steel—as soothing
As a child's rhyme—

Merge him in the ancient music
Of all who have ever mown
Swathes in a flowery meadow
With scythe and stone.

ARTHUR WOLSELEY RUSSELL

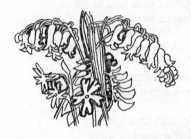

skewbald: some black, some white

✢ Charley Lee

A low moon shone on the desert land and the sage was silver
    white,
As Lee—a thong round hand and hand—stood straight in
    the lantern light.
'You have strung up Red and Burke,' said he,
'And you say that the next will be Charley Lee,
But there's never a rope was made for me.'
And he laughed in the quiet night.

They shaped the noose and they flicked the rope and over
    the limb it fell,
And Charley Lee saw the ghost of hope go glimmering
    down to hell,
Two shadows swung from the cottonwood tree,
And the wind went whispering, 'Charley Lee,'
For the turning shadows would soon be three,
And never a stone to tell.

'Have ye more to say for yourself?' said Gray, 'a message
    the like, or prayer?
If ye have, then hasten and have your say. We trailed and
    we trapped ye fair,
With fire and iron at Hidden Sink,
Where none but the stolen horses drink.
And the chain but wanted a final link.
Ye were riding my red roan mare.'

'But prove your property first,' said Lee. 'Would you call
    the mare your own,
With never a brand or mark to see, or name to the big red
    roan?
But strip the saddle and turn her loose,
And I'll show that the mare is my own cayuse.
And I don't—then take it a fair excuse,
To tighten the rope you've thrown.'

Gaunt, grim faces and steady eyes were touched with a
    sombre look,
And hands slipped slowly to belted thighs and held on a
    finger-crook,
For Gray of Mesa who claimed the mare,
Had talked too much as he led them there,
Nor other among them knew the lair,
So a grip on their haste they took.

'Give him a chance,' said Monty Wade, and, 'What is the
    use?' said Blake.
'He's done,' said Harney; 'his string is played. But we'll
    give him an even break.'
So they led the mare to the cottonwood tree,
Nor saddle nor bridle nor rope had she.
'Bonnie, come here!' said Charley Lee,
And soft was the word he spake.

The roan mare came and she nosed his side and nuzzled
    him friendly-wise;
'Kneel!' cried Lee, and he leaped astride and fled as the
    swallow flies.
Flashes followed his flight in vain,
Bullets spattered the ground like rain,
Hoofs drummed far on the midnight plain,
And a low moon rode the skies.

Dawn broke red on the desert land where the turning
    shadows fell,
And the wind drove over the rolling sand with a whimper-
    ing ebb and swell,
Whimpering, whispering, 'Charley Lee,'
As south on the red roan mare rode he,
Yet the turning shadows they were three,
And never a stone to tell.

HENRY HERBERT KNIBBS

❧ The Towerer

Old Jarge, Hal, Walter and I, the Rector and Bill,
The old red setter and Joe, the retriever, Bess,
Went out in the cider time for something to kill,
Past Arthur's Camp, a couple of miles, I guess.

We came in the noon of the blue September day
To a tongue of grass thrust into a cleft of copse,
Berries were black and plump on the changing spray,
A dwindled spring went over its lip in drops.

We stopped to drink at the spring, Hal, Walter and I,
The retriever, Bess, the old red setter and Joe.
A covey went up with a whirr and the guns let fly,
The birds went skimming the trees towards Barney's Low.

They fired two last long shots, the Rector and Bill,
A feather came out of a bird, but the bird went on.
'Hit him,' they said; we muttered, 'You didn't kill.'
Over the tips of the trees the covey was gone.

The hit bird swerved from the line of the covey's charge,
Over the grass of the field we watched him rise:
'Got him,' the Rector said. 'Her towers,' said Jarge.
We saw him breast like a lark the hot blue skies.

He climbed the air till he struggled in sky alone,
Straining and beating up on a battling breast,
Then paused, then dropped with a thump upon bounding
    bone:
Joe brought him in; we bagged him up with the rest.

At covey-call time in the dusk September eve,
We loitered home together and shared the kill:
Nine brace, three rabbits, a hare: we all took leave;
Jarge took the dogs: the moon came over the hill.

Poor Bess, the retriever died, her muzzle all white;
A run-away cart ran over the spaniel, Joe;
Jarge died of a quart of rum next Christmas night;
The old red setter went west, oh, ages ago.

Bill died from shock of a fall, as his heart was weak,
The rector lingered to die of a sheer old age;
Walter went down with a stroke and could not speak,
He, too, has gathered his goods and drawn his wage.

Only Hal and myself of the nine remain,
And Hal's forgotten the bird, forgotten the shoot;
The grass, the wood and the spring are here in my brain,
With the dogs and the wine-leaved brambles black with fruit.

I think of the towering bird with its choking lung,
Its bursting heart, its struggle to scale the sky,
And wonder when we shall all be tried and hung
For the blue September crime when we made it die.

JOHN MASEFIELD

❧ Water-Finders

Old Hall the ashes from his pipe knocked out,
Blew through it, then he said: 'You've asked about
These water-finders, sir. There's two I knows
And uses, when on building-jobs I goes:
They've found me many a spring. John Forde of Noke,
The blacksmith—he's a tall man, tough as oak—
He *fights* against the power with all his might;
He holds his hands out *so*, with sinews tight.
And yet, for all that he's so strong and big,
The power's that fierce, I've seen a hazel-twig
Twist all askew, when in his fingers gripped,
Tugged earthward! Though he held it fast it slipped!
And, when the spring's beneath, his muscles *swell*—
You'd not believe me, if I was to tell!
That's why he's grown so strong and large of arm—
For he's a great stout man, and takes no harm.

'T'other's a different sort. You've heard, perhaps,
Of Islip Tom? He's one of these small chaps,
And *weak*. He cannot fight the power—he shakes,
He lets it *slide* over his arms, and takes
The shock deep in his breast; and people say
This water-work will be his death one day.
He's grown *that* weak—his chest is all sunk in,
His face is sharp, his arms are dry and thin.
He shudders when the current hits his heart;
The sweat runs from his head, his eyeballs start.
And that's why when I has him for the job,
I always pays an extra couple of bob.'

EDWARD THOMPSON

❧ Christmas at Sea

The sheets were frozen hard, and they cut the naked hand;
The decks were like a slide, where a seaman scarce could
    stand;
The wind was a nor'-wester, blowing squally off the sea;
And cliffs and spouting breakers were the only things a-lee.

They heard the surf a-roaring before the break of day;
But 'twas only with the peep of light we saw how ill we lay.
We tumbled every hand on deck instanter, with a shout,
And we gave her the maintops'l, and stood by to go about.

All day we tack'd and tack'd between the South Head and
    the North;
All day we haul'd the frozen sheets, and got no further
    forth;
All day as cold as charity, in bitter pain and dread,
For very life and nature we tack'd from head to head.

We gave the South a wider berth, for there the tide-race
    roar'd;
But every tack we made we brought the North Head close
    aboard;
So's we saw the cliffs and houses, and the breakers running
    high,
And the coastguard in his garden, with his glass against
    his eye.

The frost was on the village roofs as white as ocean foam;
The good red fires were burning bright in every 'longshore
    home;
The windows sparkled clear, and the chimneys volley'd out;
And I vow we sniff'd the victuals as the vessel went about.

The bells upon the church were rung with a mighty jovial
  cheer;
For it's just that I should tell you how (of all days in the
  year)
This day of our adversity was blessed Christmas morn,
And the house above the coastguard's was the house where
  I was born.

O well I saw the pleasant room, the pleasant faces there,
My mother's silver spectacles, my father's silver hair;
And well I saw the firelight, like a flight of homely elves
Go dancing round the china plates that stand upon the
  shelves!

And well I knew the talk they had, the talk that was of me,
Of the shadow on the household and the son that went to
  sea;
And O the wicked fool I seem'd, in every kind of way,
To be here and hauling frozen ropes on blessed Christmas
  Day.

They lit the high sea-light, and the dark began to fall.
'All hands to loose topgallant sails!' I heard the Captain
  call.
'By the Lord, she'll never stand it,' our first mate Jackson
  cried.
'. . . It's the one way or the other, Mr Jackson,' he replied.

She stagger'd to her bearings, but the sails were new and
  good,
And the ship smelt up to windward just as though she
  understood.
As the winter's day was ending, in the entry of the night,
We clear'd the weary headland, and passed below the light.

And they heaved a mighty breath, every soul on board
  but me,
As they saw her nose again pointing handsome out to sea;
But all that I could think of, in the darkness and the cold,
Was just that I was leaving home and my folks were growing
  old.

ROBERT LOUIS STEVENSON

✂ The Plodder Seam

The Plodder Seam is a wicked seam,
It's worse than the Trencherbone.
It's hot and there's three foot of shale between
The coal and the rocky stone.
You can smell the smoke from the fires of hell
Deep under Ashton town.
Oh, the Plodder Seam is a wicked seam,
It's a mile and a quarter down.

Thirteen hundred tons a day
Are taken from that mine.
There's a ton of dirt for a ton of coal,
And a gallon of sweat and grime.
We crawl behind the cutters and
We scrabble for the coal.
Oh, I'd rather sweep the street than have
To burrow like a mole.

ANON.

❧ The Ballad of the
Tinker's Daughter

When rooks ripped home at eventide
And trees pegged shadows to the ground,
The tinkers came to Carhan bridge
And camped beside the Famine mound.

With long-eared ass and bony horse,
And blue-wheeled cart and caravan,
And she, the fairest of them all,
The daughter of the tinker clan.

The sun flamed in her red, red hair,
And in her eyes danced stars of mirth,
Her body held the willow's grace,
Her feet scarce touched the springing earth.

The night spread its star-tasselled shawls,
The river gossiped to its stones,
She sat beside the leaping fire
And sang the songs the tinker owns.

The songs as old as turning wheels
And sweet as bird-throats after rain,
Deep wisdom of the wild wet earth,
The pain of joy, the joy of pain.

A farmer going by the road
To tend his cattle in the byre
Saw her like some fairy queen
Between the river and the fire.

Her beauty stirred his brooding blood,
Her magic mounted in his head,
He stole her from her tinker clan
And on the morrow they were wed.

And when the sunlight swamped the hills
And bird-song drowned the river's bells,
The tinkers quenched their hazel fires
And climbed the windy road to Kells.

And from his house she watched them go
With blue-wheeled cart and caravan,
The long-eared ass and bony horse,
And brown-haired woman and tinker man.

She watched them go, she watched them fade
And vanish in the yellow furze;
A cold wind blew across the sun
And silenced all the singing birds.

She saw the months run on and on,
And heard the river fret and foam,
At white of day the roosters called,
At dim of dusk the cows came home.

The crickets strummed their heated harps
In hidden halls behind the hob
And told of distant waterways
Where the black moorhens dive and bob

And shoot the glassy bubbles up
To smash their windows on the stones;
And brown trout hide their spots of gold
Among the river's pebbly bones;

And, too, the ebbing sea that flung
A net of sound about the stars
Set strange hills dancing in her dreams
And meshed her to the wandering cars.

She stole out from her sleeping man
And fled the fields that tied her down,
Her face moved towards the rising sun,
Her back was to the tired town.

She climbed the pallid road to Kells,
Against the hill, against the wind,
In Glenbeigh of the mountain-streams
She came among her tinker-kind.

They bedded her between the wheels
And there her son was born,
She heard the tinker-woman's praise
Before she died that morn. . . .

The years flew by like frightened birds
That spill a feather and are gone,
The farmer walked his weedful fields
And made the tinkers travel on.

No more they camped by Carhan bridge
And coaxed their fires to fragrant flame,
They saw him with his dog and gun,
They spat and cursed his name.

And when May hid the hawthorn trees
With stars she stole from out the skies
There came a barefoot tinker lad
With red, red hair and laughing eyes.

He left the road, he crossed the fields,
The farmer shot him in the side,
The smile went from his twisting lips,
He told his name and died.

That evening when the neighbours came
They found the son laid on the floor,
And saw the father swinging dead
Between the window and the door.

They placed the boy upon the cart
And cut the swaying farmer down,
They swear a tinker-woman came
With them all the way to town.

The sun flamed in her red, red hair,
And in her eyes danced stars of mirth,
Her body held the willow's grace
Her feet scarce touched the springing earth.

They buried them in Keelvarnogue
And eyes were moist and lips were wan,
And when the mound was patted down
The tinker maid was gone.

These things were long before my day,
I only speak with borrowed words,
But that is how the story goes
In Iveragh of the singing birds.

SIGERSON CLIFFORD

✣ Adlestrop

Yes. I remember Adlestrop—
The name, because one afternoon
Of heat the express-train drew up there
Unwontedly. It was late June.

The steam hissed. Some one cleared his throat.
No one left and no one came
On the bare platform. What I saw
Was Adlestrop—only the name

And willows, willow-herb, and grass,
And meadowsweet, and haycocks dry,
No whit less still and lonely fair
Than the high cloudlets in the sky.

And for that minute a blackbird sang
Close by, and round him, mistier,
Farther and farther, all the birds
Of Oxfordshire and Gloucestershire.

EDWARD THOMAS

꩜ Ticonderoga

On the loch sides of Appin,
When the mist blew from the sea,
A Stewart stood with a Cameron;
An angry man was he.
The blood beat in his ears,
The blood ran hot to head,
The mist blew from the sea,
And there was the Cameron dead.

'O, what have I done to my friend,
O, what have I done to mysel',
That he should be cold and dead,
And I in the danger of all?

'Nothing but danger about me,
Danger behind and before,
Death at wait in the heather,
In Appin and Mamore,
Hate at all of the ferries
And death at each of the fords,
Camerons priming gunlocks
And Camerons sharpening swords.'

But this was a man of counsel,
This was a man of a score,
There dwelt no pawkier Stewart
In Appin or Mamore.
He looked on the blowing mist,
He looked on the awful dead,
And there came a smile on his face
And there slipped a thought in his head.

78

Out over cairn and moss,
Out over scrog and scaur,
He ran as runs the clansman
That bears the cross of war.
His heart beat in his body,
His hair clove to his face,
When he came at last in the gloaming
To the dead man's brother's place.
The east was white with the moon,
The west with the sun was red,
And there, in the house-doorway,
Stood the brother of the dead.

'I have slain a man to my danger,
I have slain a man to my death.
I put my soul in your hands,'
The panting Stewart saith.
'I lay it bare in your hands,
For I know your hands are leal;
And be you my targe and bulwark
From the bullet and the steel.'

Then up and spoke the Cameron,
And gave him his hand again:
'There shall never a man in Scotland
Set faith in me in vain;
And whatever man you have slaughtered,
Of whatever name or line,
By my sword and yonder mountain,
I make your quarrel mine.
I bid you in to my fireside,
I share with you house and hall;
It stands upon my honour
To see you safe from all.'

79

It fell in the time of midnight,
When the fox barked in the den,
And the plaids were over the faces
In all the houses of men,
That as the living Cameron
Lay sleepless on his bed,
Out of the night and the other world,
Came in to him the dead.

'My blood is on the heather,
My bones are on the hill;
There is joy in the home of ravens
That the young shall eat their fill.
My blood is poured in the dust,
My soul is spilled in the air;
And the man that has undone me
Sleeps in my brother's care.'

'I'm wae for your death, my brother,
But if all of my house were dead,
I couldnae withdraw the plighted hand
Nor break the word once said.'

'O what shall I say to our father,
In the place to which I fare?
O, what shall I say to our mother,
Who greets to see me there?
And to all the kindly Camerons
That have lived and died long-syne—
Is this the word you send them,
Fause-hearted brother mine?'

'It's neither fear nor duty,
It's neither quick nor dead
Shall gar me withdraw the plighted hand,
Or break the word once said.'

Thrice in the time of midnight,
When the fox barked in the den,
And the plaids were over the faces
In all the houses of men,
Thrice as the living Cameron
Lay sleepless on his bed,
Out of the night and the other world
Came in to him the dead,
And cried to him for vengeance
On the man that laid him low;
And thrice the living Cameron
Told the dead Cameron, no.

'Thrice have you seen me, brother,
But now shall see me no more,
Till you meet your angry fathers
Upon the farther shore.
Thrice have I spoken, and now,
Before the cock be heard,
I take my leave for ever
With the naming of a word.
It shall sing in your sleeping ears,
It shall hum in your waking head,
The name—Ticonderoga,
And the warning of the dead.'

THE PLACE OF THE NAME

There fell a war in a woody place
Lay far across the sea,
A war of the march in the mirk midnight
And the shot from behind the tree,
The shaven head and the painted face,
The silent foot in the wood,
In a land of a strange, outlandish tongue
That was hard to be understood.

81

It fell about the gloaming
The general stood with his staff,
He stood and he looked east and west
With little mind to laugh.

'Far have I been and much have I seen,
And kent both gain and loss,
But here we have woods on every hand
And a kittle water to cross.
Far have I been and much have I seen,
But never the beat of this;
And there's one must go down to that waterside
To see how deep it is.'

It fell in the dusk of the night
When unco things betide,
The skilly captain, the Cameron,
Went down to that waterside.
Canny and soft the captain went;
And a man of the woody land,
With shaven head and the painted face
Went down at his right hand.
It fell in the quiet night,
There was never a sound to ken;
But all of the woods to the right and the left
Lay filled with the painted men.

'Far have I been and much have I seen
Both as a man and boy,
But never have I set forth a foot
On so perilous an employ.'
It fell in the dusk of the night
When unco things betide,
That he was aware of a captain-man
Drew near to the waterside.
He was aware of his coming

Down in the gloaming alone;
And he looked in the face of the man
And lo! the face was his own.

'This is my weird,' he said,
'And now I ken the worst;
For many shall fall the morn,
But I shall fall with the first,
O, you of the outland tongue,
You of the painted face,
This is the place of death;
Can you tell me the name of the place?'

'Since the Frenchmen have been here
They have called it Sault-Marie;
But that is a name for priests,
And not for you and me.
It went by another word,'
Quoth he of the shaven head:
'It was called Ticonderoga
In the days of the great dead.'

And it fell on the morrow's morning,
In the fiercest of the fight,
That the Cameron bit the dust
As he foretold at night;
And far from the hills of heather,
Far from the isles of the sea,
He sleeps in the place of the name,
As it was doomed to be.

ROBERT LOUIS STEVENSON

pawkier: more artful   *scrog*: moor   *scaur*: cliff   *leal*: loyal
greets: weeps   *wae*: sorrowful   *gar*: make   *kittle*: difficult
unco: uncanny   *weird*: fate

Ticonderoga lies in the north-east corner of New York State. At one time it was a fort built and garrisoned by the French. It was captured in 1759 by the British.

ᔦᔋ Spanish Waters

Spanish Waters, Spanish waters, you are ringing in my ears
Like a slow sweet piece of music from the grey forgotten
  years;
Telling tales, and beating tunes, and bringing weary
  thoughts to me
Of the sandy beach at Muertos, where I would that I
  could be.

There's a surf breaks on Los Muertos, and it never stops
  to roar,
And it's there we came to anchor, and it's there we went
  ashore,
Where the blue lagoon is silent amid snags of rotting trees,
Dropping like the clothes of corpses cast up by the seas.

We anchored at Los Muertos when the dipping sun was red,
We left her half-a-mile to sea, to west of Nigger Head;
And before the mist was on the Cay, before the day was
  done,
We were all ashore on Muertos with the gold that we had
  won.

We bore it through the marshes in a half-score battered
  chests,
Sinking, in the sucking quagmires to the sunburn on our
  breasts,
Heaving over tree-trunks, gasping, damning at the flies
  and heat,
Longing for a long drink, out of silver, in the ship's cool
  lazareet.

The moon came white and ghostly as we laid the treasure
down,
There was gear there'd make a beggarman as rich as Lima
Town,
Copper charms and silver trinkets from the chests of
Spanish crews,
Gold doubloons and double moidores, louis d'ors and
portagues,

Clumsy yellow-metal earrings from the Indians of Brazil,
Uncut emeralds out of Rio, bezoar stones from Guayaquil;
Silver, in the crude and fashioned, pots of old Arica bronze,
Jewels from the bones of Incas desecrated by the Dons.

We smoothed the place with mattocks, and we took and
blazed the tree,
Which marks yon where the gear is hid that none will ever
see,
And we laid aboard the ship again, and south away we
steers,
Through the loud surf of Los Muertos which is beating in
my ears.

I'm the last alive that knows it. All the rest have gone
their ways
Killed, or died, or come to anchor in the old Mulatas Cays,
And I go singing, fiddling, old and starved and in despair,
And I know where all that gold is hid, if I were only there.

It's not the way to end it all. I'm old, and nearly blind,
And an old man's past's a strange thing, for it never leaves
his mind.
And I see in dreams, awhiles, the beach, the sun's disc
dipping red,
And the tall ship, under topsails, swaying in past Nigger
Head.

I'd be glad to step ashore there. Glad to take a pick and go
To the lone blazed coco-palm tree in the place no others
know,
And lift the gold and silver that has mouldered there for
years
By the loud surf of Los Muertos which is beating in my
ears.

JOHN MASEFIELD

lazareet: storeroom

ᗡᖇ Old Christmas

'Where you coming from, Lomey Carter,
    So early over the snow?
What's them pretties you got in your hand,
    And where you aiming to go?

Step in, Honey. Old Christmas morning
    We hain't got nothing much;
Maybe a bite of sweetness and corn bread,
    A little ham meat and such.

But come in, Lomey. Sally Ann Barton's
    Hungering after your face.
Wait till I light my candle up.
    Set down. There's your old place.

Where you been, so early this morning?'
    'Grave yard, Sally Ann:
Up by the trace in the Salt Lick meadow
    Where Taulbe kilt my man.'

'Taulbe hain't to home this morning.
    Wisht I could scratch me a light:
Dampness gits in the heads of the matches;
    I'll blow up the embers bright.'

'Needn't trouble. I won't be stopping:
    Going a long ways still.'
'You didn't see nothing, Lomey Carter,
    Up on the grave yard hill?'

'What should I see there, Sally Ann Barton?'
  'Spirits walk loose last night.'
'There was an elder bush a blooming
  While the moon still give some light.'

'Yes, elder bushes they bloom, Old Christmas,
  And critters kneel down in their straw.
Anything else? Up in the graveyard?'
  'One thing more I saw:

I saw my man with his head all bleeding
  Where Taulbe's shot went through.'
'What did he say?' 'He stooped and kissed me.'
  'What did he say to you?'

'Said Lord Jesus forgive your Taulbe;
  But he told me another word;
Said it soft when he stooped and kissed me;
  That was the last I heard.'

'Taulbe hain't come home this morning.'
  'I know that, Sally Ann,
For I kilt him, coming down through the meadow
  Where Taulbe kilt my man.

I met him up on the meadow trace
  When the moon was fainting fast;
I had my dead man's rifle gun,
  And kilt him as he come past.'

'I heard two shots.' ' 'Twas his was second:
   He got me 'fore he died.
You'll find us at daybreak, Sally Ann Barton:
   I'm laying there dead at his side.'

ROY HELTON

trace: edge
salt-lick: salt-lake

This poem is a ballad of the Kentucky Mountains, an area noted
for its feuding families, superstitions, and ghosts. Some of these
superstitions centre round Old Christmas (January 6th), or
Twelfth Night as it is sometimes called—the blooming of the
elder bush, for instance, and ghostly visitations.

❧ On the Swag

His body doubled
   under the pack
   that sprawls untidily
   on his old back
   the cold wet deadbeat
   plods up the track.

The cook peers out:
   'Oh curse that old lag
   here again
   with his clumsy swag
   made of a dirty old
   turnip bag.'

'Bring him in, cook,
   from the grey level sleet,
   put silk on his body,
   slippers on his feet,
   give him fire
   and bread and meat.

'Let the fruit be plucked
   and the cake be iced,
   the bed be snug
   and the wine be spiced
   in the old cove's nightcap
   For this is Christ.'

R. A. K. MASON

deadbeat: tramp
swag: kitbag

❦ Tarantella

Do you remember an Inn,
Miranda?
Do you remember an Inn?
And the tedding and the spreading
Of the straw for a bedding,
And the fleas that tease in the High Pyrenees,
And the wine that tasted of the tar?
And the cheers and the jeers of the young muleteers
(Under the dark of the vine verandah)?
Do you remember an Inn, Miranda,
Do you remember an Inn?
And the cheers and the jeers of the young muleteers
Who hadn't got a penny,
And who weren't paying any,
And the hammer at the doors and the Din?
And the Hip! Hop! Hap!
Of the clap
Of the hands to the twirl and the swirl
Of the girls gone chancing,
Glancing,
Dancing,
Backing and advancing,
Snapping of the clapper to the spin
Out and in—
And the Ting, Tong, Tang of the guitar!
Do you remember an Inn,
Miranda?
Do you remember an Inn?

Never more;
Miranda,
Never more.
Only the high peaks hoar:
And Aragon a torrent at the door.

No sound
In the walls of the Halls where falls
The tread
Of the feet of the dead to the ground.
No sound:
Only the boom
Of the far Waterfall like Doom.

HILAIRE BELLOC

Hilaire Belloc wrote this poem in 1929 for a girl named Miranda
Mackintosh, the daughter of a friend: but many people believe
that in the first part of the poem, with its wonderful reproduction
of the rhythm of the Spanish dance, he is recalling carefree holiday
occasions in Spain with his wife, Elodie, to whom he was extremely
devoted; and that the final part recalls her untimely death in 1913.

❧ The Blind Girl

He never talked about the present
Because it had vanished
For him, as well as for her,
When his daughter went blind.
She could play with the flowers, but could never know their
    colours,
This child with her dark and lustrous eyes,
Regarding you, looking seriously, and seeing nothing.
As she talked, her gaze would remain level
And she would feel the shape of a flower with her fingers
Loving it, as her father loved it with his eyes.

OSBERT SITWELL

✣ The Old Man and Jim

Old man never had much to say—
'Ceptin' to Jim,—
And Jim was the wildest boy he had—
And the old man jes' wrapped up in him!
Never heerd him speak but once
Er twice in my life,—and first time was
When the army broke out, and Jim he went,
The old man backin' him, fer three months:
And all 'at I heerd the old man say
Was, jes' as we turned to start away,—
'Well, goodbye, Jim:
Take keer of yourse'f!'

'Peared-like, he was more satisfied
Jes' lookin' at Jim
And likin' him all to hisse'f-like, see?—
'Cause he was jes' wrapped up in him!
And over and over I mind the day
The old man come and stood round in the way
While we was drillin', a-watchin' Jim—
And down at the deepot a-heerin' him say,
'Well, goodbye, Jim
Take keer of yourse'f!'

Never was nothin' about the farm
Disting'ished Jim;
Neighbours all used to wonder why
The old man 'peared wrapped up in him:
But when Cap. Biggler he writ back
'At Jim was the bravest boy we had
In the whole dern regiment, white er black,
And his fightin' good as his farmin' bad—
'At he had led, with a bullet clean

Bored through his thigh, and carried the flag
Through the bloodiest battle you ever seen.—
The old man wound up a letter to him
'At Cap. read to us, 'at said: 'Tell Jim goodbye,
And take keer of hisse'f.'

Jim come home jes' long enough
To take the whim
'At he'd like to go back in the cavalry—
And the old man jes' wrapped up in him!
Jim 'lowed 'at he'd had sich luck afore,
Guessed he'd tackle her three years more.
And the old man give him a colt he'd raised,
And follered him over to Camp Ben Wade,
And laid around fer a week or so,
Watchin' Jim on dress-parade—
Till finally he rid away,
And last he heerd was the old man say,—
'Well, goodbye, Jim:
Take keer of yourse'f!'

Tuk the papers, the old man did,
A-watchin' fer Jim—
Fully believin' he'd make his mark
Some way—jes' wrapped up in him!—
And many a time the word 'u'd come
'At stirred him up like the tap of a drum—
At Petersburg, fer instance, where
Jim rid right into their cannons there,
And tuk them, and pointed them t'other way,
And socked it home to the boys in grey,
As they scooted fer timber, and on and on—
Jim a lieutenant and one arm gone,
And the old man's words in his mind all day,—
'Well, goodbye, Jim:
Take keer of yourse'f!'

Think of a private, now, perhaps,
We'll say like Jim,
'At's climbed clean up to the shoulder-straps—
And the old man jes' wrapped up in him!
Think of him—with the war plum' through,
And the glorious old Red-White-and-Blue
A-laughin' the news down over Jim,
And the old man bendin' over him—
The surgeon turnin' away with tears
'At hadn't leaked for years and years,
As the hand of the dyin' boy clung to
His father's, the old voice in his ears,—
'Well, goodbye, Jim:
Take keer of yourse'f!'

JAMES WHITCOMB RILEY

✤ Ask and Have

'Oh, 'tis time I should talk to your mother,
Sweet Mary,' says I.
'Oh, don't talk to my mother,' says Mary,
Beginning to cry:
'For my mother says men are deceivers,
And never, I know, will consent;
She says girls in a hurry who marry,
At leisure repent.'

'Then, suppose I would talk to your father,
Sweet Mary,' says I.
'Oh, don't talk to my father,' says Mary,
Beginning to cry:
'For my father he loves me so dearly,
He'll never consent I should go—
If you talk to my father,' says Mary,
'He'll surely say, "No".'

'Then how shall I get you, my jewel?
Sweet Mary,' says I;
'If your father and mother's so cruel,
Most surely I'll die.'
'Oh, never say die, dear,' says Mary;
'A way now to save you I see:
Since my parents are both so contrary—
You'd better ask me!'

SAMUEL LOVER

೫ The Mountain Still

I THE MOONSHINER

He leans far out and watches: down below
The road seems but a ribbon through the trees:
The bluff, from which he gazes, whence he sees
Some ox-team or some horseman come and go,
Is briered with brush. A man comes riding slow
Around a bend of road. Against his knees
The branches whip. He sits at careless ease.
It is the sheriff, armed for any foe.
A detonation tears the echoes from
Each pine-hung crag; upon the rider's brow
A smear of red springs out; he shades it now,
His grey eyes on the bluff. The crags are dumb.
Smoke wreathes one spot. The sheriff, with a cough,
Marks well that place, and then rides slowly off.

II THE SHERIFF

Night and the mountain road: a crag where burns
What seems a star, low down: three men that glide
From tree and rock towards it; one a guide
For him who never from his purpose turns,
Who stands for law among these mountain kerns.
At last the torchlit cave, along whose side
The still is seen, and men who have defied
The law so long—law, whom the threshold spurns
With levelled weapons now . . . Wolves in a den
Fight not more fiercely than these fought; wild fear
In every face, and rage and pale surprise.
The smoke thins off, and in the cave four men
Lie dead or dying; one that mountaineer,
And one the sheriff with the fearless eyes.

MADISON CAWEIN

kerns: peasants

99

The Ponies

During the strike, the ponies were brought up
From their snug stables, some three hundred feet
Below the surface—up the pit's main shaft
Shot one by one into the light of day;
And as each stepped, bewildered, from the cage,
He stood among his fellows, shivering
In the unaccustomed freshness of free air,
His dim eyes dazzled by the April light.
And then one suddenly left the huddled group,
Lifted his muzzle, sniffed the freshness in,
Pawed the soft turf and, whinnying, started trotting
Across the field; and one by one his fellows
With pricking ears each slowly followed him,
Timidly trotting: when the leader's trot
Broke into a canter, then into a gallop;
And now the whole herd galloped at his heels
Around the dewy meadow, hard hoofs, used
To stumbling over treacherous stony tramways
And plunging hock-deep through black steamy puddles
Of the dark narrow galleries, delighting
In the soft spring of the resilient turf,
Still round and round the field they raced, unchecked
By tugging traces, at their heels no longer
The trundling tubs, and round and round and round,
With a soft thunder of hoofs, the sunshine flashing
On their sleek coats, through the bright April weather
They raced all day: and even when the night
Kindled clear stars above them in a sky
Strangely unsullied by the stack which now
No longer belched out blackness, still they raced,
Unwearied, as through their short sturdy limbs
The rebel blood like wildfire ran, their lungs
Filled with the breath of freedom. On they sped
Through the sweet dewy darkness; and all night

The watchman at the pithead heard the thudding
Of those careering and exultant hoofs
Still circling in a crazy chase; and dawn
Found them still steaming raggedly around,
Tailing into a lagging cantering,
And so to a stumbling trot: when gradually
Dropping out one by one, they started cropping
The dew-dark tender grass, which no foul reek
From the long idle pit now smirched, and drinking
With quivering nostrils the rich living breath
Of sappy growing things, the cool rank green
Grateful to eyes, familiar from their colthood
Only with darkness and the dusty glimmer
Of lamplit galleries. . . .
May hap one day
Our masters, too, will go on strike, and we
Escape the dark and drudgery of the pit,
And race unreined around the fields of heaven!

W. W. GIBSON

✨ The Witch

'I have walked a great while over the snow,
And I am not tall nor strong.
My clothes are wet, and my teeth are set,
And the way was hard and long.
I have wandered over the fruitful earth,
But I never came here before.
O lift me over the threshold, and let me in at the door!

'The cutting wind is a cruel foe.
I dare not stand in the blast.
My hands are stone, and my voice a groan,
And the worst of death is past.
I am but a little maiden still,
My little white feet are sore.
O lift me over the threshold, and let me in at the door!'

Her voice was the voice that women have,
Who plead for their heart's desire.
She came—she came—and the quivering flame
Sank and died in the fire.
It never was lit again on my hearth
Since I hurried across the floor,
To lift her over the threshold, and let her in at the door.

MARY E. COLERIDGE

The Ballad of Billy Rose

Outside Bristol Rovers Football Ground—
The date has gone from me, but not the day,
Nor how dissenting flags in stiff array
Struck bravely out against the grey sky's round—

Near the Car Park then, past Austin and Ford,
Lagonda, Bentley, and a colourful patch
Of country coaches come in for the match
Was where I walked, having travelled the road

From Fishponds to watch Portsmouth in the Cup.
The Third Round, I believe. And I was filled
With the old excitement which had thrilled
Me so completely when, while growing up,

I went on Saturdays to match or fight.
Not only me; for thousands of us there
Strode forward eagerly, each man aware
Of tingling memory, anticipating delight.

We all marched forward, all except one man.
I saw him because he was paradoxically still,
A stone against the flood, face upright against us all,
Head bare, hoarse voice aloft. Blind as a stone.

I knew him at once despite his pathetic clothes;
Something in his stance, or his sturdy frame
Perhaps. I would even remember his name
Before I saw it on his blind-man's tray. Billy Rose.

And twenty forgetful years fell away at the sight.
Bare-kneed, dismayed, memory fled to the hub
Of Saturday violence, with friends to the Labour Club
Watching the boxing on a sawdust summer night.

The boy's enclosure close to the shabby ring
Was where we stood, clenched in a resin world,
Spoke in cool voices, lounged, were artificially bored
During minor bouts. We paid threepence to go in.

Billy Rose fought there. He was top of the bill.
So brisk a fighter, so gallant, so precise!
Trim as a tree he stood for the ceremonies,
Then turned to meet George Morgan of Tirphil.

He had no chance. Courage was not enough,
Nor tight defence. Donald Davies was sick—
We threatened his cowardice with an embarrassed kick.
Ripped across both his eyes was Rose, but we were tough

And clapped him as they wrapped his blindness up
In busy towels, applauded the wave
He gave his executioners, cheered the brave
Blind man as he cleared with a jaunty hop

The top rope. I had forgotten that day
As if it were dead for ever, yet now I saw
The flowers of punched blood on the ring floor,
As bright as his name. I do not know

How long I stood with ghosts of the wild fists
And the cries of shaken boys long dead around me,
For struck to act at last, in terror and pity
I threw some frantic money, three treacherous pence

(I cry at the memory) into his tray, and ran,
Entering the waves of the stadium like a drowning man.
Poor Billy Rose. God, he could fight
Before my three sharp coins knocked out his sight.

LESLIE NORRIS

104

✹ The Visionary

A witch doctor treated him for trachoma
funnelling the dry powdered root,
more caustic than mustard gas,
into each brown, red-haloed pupil.

The lances ran through to rest
on the back of his skull for a few weeks
after he had stumbled, numb, speechless
groping even the ground with hands
individually terrified of scorpions, home.

For two years he sat in the doorway
while his wives ministered beer,
mealie-meal, sometimes meat,
avoiding in a half circle his blind stare.

One night he followed something alone,
spouses and progeny snoring unaware,
not bothering to wake the small child
that led him tetherlike on a stick,
fell into a dry well and died upside down.

DOUGLAS LIVINGSTONE

trachoma: eye disease

✒ Squire Hooper

Hooper was ninety. One September dawn
He sent a messenger
For his physician, who asked thereupon
What ailed the sufferer
Which he might circumvent, and promptly bid begone.

'Doctor, I summoned you,' the squire replied—
'Pooh-pooh me though you may—
To ask what's happened to me—burst inside,
It seems—not much, I'd say—
But awkward with a house-full here for a shoot today.'

And he described the symptoms. With bent head
The listener looked grave.
'H'm ... *You're a dead man in six hours*,' he said.
'I speak out, since you are brave—
And best 'tis you should know, that last things be sped.'

'Right,' said the squire. 'And now comes—what to do?
One thing: on no account
Must I now spoil the sport I've asked them to—
My guests are paramount—
They must scour scrub and stubble; and big bags bring as
  due.'

He downed to breakfast, and bespoke his guests:—
'I find I have to go
An unexpected journey, and it rests
With you, my friends, to show
The shoot can go off gaily, whether I'm there or no.'

Thus blandly spoke he; and to the fields they went,
And Hooper up the stair.
They had a glorious day; and stiff and spent
Returned as dusk drew near.—
'Gentlemen,' said the doctor, 'he's not back as meant,

To his deep regret!'—So they took leave, each guest
Observing: 'I dare say
Business detains him in the town: 'tis best
We should no longer stay
Just now. We'll come again anon'; and they went their way.

Meeting two men in the obscurity
Shouldering a box, a thin
Cloth-covering wrapt, one sportsman cried: 'Damn me,
I thought them carrying in,
At first, a coffin; till I knew it could not be.'

THOMAS HARDY

❧ When Mary Thro' the Garden Went

When Mary thro' the garden went,
There was no sound of any bird,
And yet, because the night was spent,
The little grasses lightly stirred,
The flowers awoke, June lilies heard.

When Mary thro' the garden went,
The dew lay still on flower and grass,
The waving palms above her sent
Their fragrance out as she did pass,
No light upon the branches was.

When Mary thro' the garden went,
Her eyes, for weeping long, were dim.
The grass beneath her footsteps bent,
The solemn lilies, white and slim,
These also stood and wept for Him.

When Mary thro' the garden went,
She sought, within the garden ground,
One for Whom her heart was rent,
One Who for her sake was bound,
One Who sought and she was found.

MARY E. COLERIDGE

❧ The Owl-Critic

'Who stuffed that white owl?' No one spoke in the shop.
The barber was busy, and he couldn't stop;
The customers, waiting their turns, were all reading
The 'Daily,' the 'Herald,' the 'Post,' little heeding
The young man who blurted out such a blunt question;
No one raised a head, or even made a suggestion;
And the barber kept on shaving.

'Don't you see, Mr. Brown,'
Cried the youth, with a frown,
'How wrong the whole thing is,
How preposterous each wing is,
How flattened the head is, how jammed down the neck is—
In short, the whole owl, what an ignorant wreck 'tis?
I make no apology;
I've learned owl-eology.

'I've passed days and nights in a hundred collections,
And cannot be blinded to any deflections
Arising from unskilful fingers that fail
To stuff a bird right, from his beak to his tail.
Mister Brown! Mister Brown!
Do take that bird down,
Or you'll soon be the laughing-stock all over town!'
And the barber kept on shaving.

'I've studied owls,
And other night-fowls,
And I tell you
What I know to be true;
An owl cannot roost
With his limbs so unloosed;
No owl in this world
Ever had his claws curled,

Ever had his legs slanted,
Ever had his bill canted,
Ever had his neck screwed
Into that attitude.
He can't *do* it, because
'Tis against all bird-laws.
An owl has a toe
That *can't* turn out so!
I've made the white owl my study for years,
And to see such a job almost moves me to tears!
Mister Brown, I'm amazed
You should be so gone crazed
As to put up a bird
In that posture absurd!
To *look* at that owl really brings on a dizziness;
The man who stuffed *him* don't half know his business!'
And the barber kept on shaving.

'With some sawdust and bark
I could stuff in the dark
An owl better than that.
I could make an old hat
Look more like an owl
Than that horrid fowl,
Stuck up there so stiff like a side of coarse leather.
In fact, about him there's not one natural feather.'

Just then, with a wink and a sly normal lurch,
The owl, very gravely, got down from his perch,
Walked and regarded his fault-finding critic
(Who thought he was stuffed) with a glance analytic,
And then fairly hooted, as if he should say:
'Your learning's at fault this time anyway;
Don't waste it again on a live bird I pray.
I'm an owl; you're another. Sir Critic, good day!'
And the barber kept on shaving.

J. T. FIELDS

✣ Return

The darkened Mess was silent. Nothing stirred.
The sounds which drifted in were muffled, blurred,
And often lost before they could be heard.
Two white-clad figures stood, without a word,
And listened to the whispering voice of night
Around the walls which hid the moon from sight.
The moonlight strayed across the hangar doors
And splashed in patches on the concrete floors;
A flarepath glimmered on the aerodrome;
The beacon flashed to guide the bombers home . . .
And then the rustling night wind brought a sound
That muttered softly, swelled and then was drowned,
And for an endless moment silence reigned,
While in the silver darkness ears were strained
To catch that long expected sound anew . . .
At last it came again, and quickly grew,
Its surging waves became a steady drone,
The world seemed filled with it, and it alone—
Gliding across the darkness overhead,
With lights at wing-tips gleaming, green and red,
The first dark shape of the returning band,
With motors throttled back, came in to land.

Now, warmly lit, the Mess was flooded through
With cheerful noise. Young men in dusty blue,
Bright scarves and heavy sweaters, eager-eyed,
Sat round the table. Everybody tried
To speak at once, and laughter strong and clear
Rang out across the room. Pint pots of beer
Were raised to thirsty lips, and once again
Nerves braced against the threat of death and pain,
Relaxed, until the things that mattered most
Were eggs and bacon, jam and buttered toast,
And these the two white figures soon supplied.

But when at last, with hunger satisfied,
They rose and stretched themselves, and made for bed,
'Where's Jimmy? I've not seen him,' someone said.
And then the talking ceased, they looked around,
As if, by seeking, Jimmy could be found.
One saw the clock. 'Still half an hour to go.
He often cuts it pretty fine, you know.'

The lights were out, the tables in the room
Once more retreated deep into the gloom.
Again the very walls were listening,
And waiting for the stealthy wind to bring
Some murmur of the last returning crew.
The curtains fluttered gently, letting through
A sudden glimpse of swiftly setting moon.
And when the shadowed ridge of Sandham Hill
Turned purple in the dawning, all too soon,
The silent room was listening, listening still.

PETER ROBERTS

⚛ Flannan Isle

Though three men dwell on Flannan Isle
To keep the lamp alight,
As we steered under the lee we caught
No glimmer through the night.

A passing ship at dawn had brought
The news, and quickly we set sail
To find out what strange thing might ail
The keepers of the deep-sea light.

The winter day broke blue and bright
With glancing sun and glancing spray
While o'er the swell our boat made way,
As gallant as a gull in flight.

But as we neared the lonely Isle
And looked up at the naked height,
And saw the lighthouse towering white
With blinded lantern that all night
Had never shot a spark
Of comfort through the dark,
So ghostly in the cold sunlight
It seemed, that we were struck the while
With wonder all too dread for words.

And, as into the tiny creek
We stole beneath the hanging crag,
We saw three queer black ugly birds—
Too big by far in my belief
For cormorant or shag—
Like seamen sitting bolt-upright
upon a half-tide reef:
But as we neared they plunged from sight,
Without a sound or spurt of white.

And still too mazed to speak,
We landed and made fast the boat
And climbed the track in single file,
Each wishing he were safe afloat,
On any sea, however far,
So be it far from Flannan Isle:
And still we seemed to climb and climb
As though we'd lost all count of time
And so must climb for evermore;
Yet all too soon we reached the door—
The black sun-blistered lighthouse door
That gaped for us ajar.

As on the threshold for a spell
We paused, we seemed to breathe the smell
Of limewash and of tar,
Familiar as our daily breath,
As though 'twere some strange scent of death;
And so yet wondering side by side
We stood a moment still tongue-tied,
And each with black foreboding eyed
The door ere we should fling it wide
To leave the sunlight for the gloom:
Till, plucking courage up, at last
Hard on each other's heels we passed
Into the living room.

Yet as we crowded through the door
We only saw a table spread
For dinner, meat and cheese and bread,
But all untouched and no one there;
As though when they sat down to eat,
Ere they could even taste,
Alarm had come and they in haste
Had risen and left the bread and meat,
For at the table-head a chair
Lay tumbled on the floor.

We listened, but we only heard
The feeble cheeping of a bird
That starved upon its perch;
And listening still, without a word
We set about our hopeless search.
We hunted high, we hunted low,
And soon ransacked the empty house;
Then o'er the Island to and fro
We ranged, to listen and to look
In every cranny, cleft or nook
That might have hid a bird or mouse:
But though we searched from shore to shore
We found no sign in any place,
And soon again stood face to face
Before the gaping door,
And stole into the room once more
As frightened children steal.
Ay, though we hunted high and low
And hunted everywhere,
Of the three men's fate we found no trace
Of any kind in any place
But a door ajar and an untouched meal
And an overtoppled chair.

And as we listened in the gloom
Of that forsaken living-room—
A chill clutch on our breath—
We thought how ill-chance came to all
Who kept the Flannan Light,
And how the rock had been the death
Of many a likely lad—
How six had come to a sudden end
And three had gone stark mad,
And one, whom we'd all known as friend,
Had leapt from the lantern one still night
And fallen dead by the lighthouse wall—

And long we thought
On the three we sought,
And of what might yet befall.

Like curs a glance has brought to heel
We listened, flinching there,
And looked and looked on the untouched meal
And the overtoppled chair.

We seemed to stand for an endless while,
Though still no word was said,
Three men alive on Flannan Isle
Who thought on three men dead.

W. W. GIBSON

Flannan Isle is a rocky, uninhabited islet off the north-west coast of Scotland beyond the Outer Hebrides with a lighthouse over 300 feet high on top of the rock. On December 15th, 1900, it was observed by passing ships that there was no light coming from the tower. On subsequent investigation it was found that the three lighthousemen had mysteriously disappeared.

🎇 The Wine Maker

It was a close-run thing, one of those operations
That relatives speak of between a hush and a sigh.
But the aged bent body, seemingly so frail,
Had a countrywoman's hardihood. One day she asked:
'Nurse, whatever's the date? The fourteenth of June?'
'No dear, the twelfth of July.' So long she had lain.
Yet at last the hospital staff, proud and marvelling,
Waved her goodbye as the family fetched her away.

Few expected her to live. They spoke with compassion:
'Let her do what she likes, it can hardly be long now—
Those things always recur.' The very next day
After her return, she decided to make some wine.
Somebody gathered rhubarb from her cottage garden,
Humouring her; but seated, she could chop it herself
Though she had to ask her sister to lift the kettle
And stow the brew away in the whitewashed larder.

There it fermented, stormily at first and then
Gently, invisibly growing stronger, while she
Thin as a new moon, on a rigorous diet,
Survived the tremulous months. . . . Three years later
Her regular visits to the hospital have tapered away,
The next is not for a twelvemonth. She's back in harness,
Almost as vigorous as twenty years ago,
Riper, though, like many a returned traveller.

Wiry, munching her gums, her eyes sagacious,
She trudges briskly about the obsolete labour
Of caring for others in a sixteenth century cottage,
Lugging jugs of water and scuttles of coal,

Cooking on oil-stoves, washing clothes in a copper.
But now she broaches her brew. It's shrewd and mellow,
A country spinster of a wine, half-sharp, half-sweet.
Time to begin this year's; the crop is ready.

ARTHUR WOLSELEY RUSSELL

✤ Men in Green

Oh, there were fifteen men in green.
Each with a tommy-gun,
Who leapt into my plane at dawn;
We rose to meet the sun.

We set our course towards the east
And climbed into the day
Till the ribbed jungle underneath
Like a giant fossil lay.

We climbed towards the distant range
Where two white paws of cloud
Clutched at the shoulders of the pass;
The green men laughed aloud.

They did not fear the ape-like cloud
That climbed the mountain crest
And hung from twisted ropes of air
With thunder in their breast.

They did not fear the summer's sun,
In whose hot centre lie
A hundred hissing cannon shells
For the unwatchful eye.

And when on Dobadura's field
We landed, each man raised
His thumb towards the open sky;
But to their right I gazed.

For fifteen men in jungle green
Rose from the kunai grass
And came towards the place. My men
In silence watched them pass;
It seemed they looked upon themselves
In Time's prophetic glass.

Oh, there were some leaned on a stick
And some on stretchers lay,
But few walked on their own two feet
In the early green of day.

They had not feared the ape-like cloud
That climbed the mountain crest;
They had not feared the summer's sun
With bullets for their breast.

Their eyes were bright, their looks were dull,
Their skin had turned to clay.
Nature had met them in the night
And stalked them in the day.

And I think still of men in green
On the Soputa track
With fifteen spitting tommy-guns
To keep a jungle back.

DAVID CAMPBELL

✒ She Moved through the Fair

My young love said to me, 'My mother won't mind,
And my father won't slight you for your lack of kind.'
Then she stepped away from me, and this she did say,
'It will not be long, love, till our wedding day.'

She stepped away from me and she went through the fair,
And fondly I watched her move here and move there,
And then she went homeward with one star awake,
As the swan in the evening moves over the lake.

Last night she came to me, my dead love came in,
So softly she came that her feet made no din;
She laid her hand on me, and this she did say,
'It will not be long, love, till our wedding day.'

ANON.

❧ The Hawk's Nest

Sierras

We checked our pace—the red road sharply rounding;
We heard the troubled flow
Of the dark olive depths of pines, resounding
A thousand feet below.

Above the tumult of the cañon lifted,
The grey hawk breathless hung;
Or on the hill a wingèd shadow drifted
Where furze and thorn-bush clung;

Or where half-way the mountain-side was furrowed
With many a seam and scar;
Or some abandoned tunnel dimly burrowed—
A mole-hill seen so far.

We looked in silence down across the distant
Unfathomable reach:
A silence broken by the guide's consistent
And realistic speech.

'Walker of Murphy's blew a hole through Peters
For telling him he lied;
Then up and dusted out of South Hornitos
Across the Long Divide.

'We ran him out of Strong's, and up through Eden,
And 'cross the ford below;
And up this cañon (Peters' brother leadin'),
And me and Clark and Joe.

'He fou't us game: somehow, I disremember
Jest how the thing kem round;
Some say 'twas wadding, some a scattered ember
From fires on the ground.

'But in one minute all the hill below him
Was just one sheet of flame;
Guardin' the crest, Sam Clark and I called to him.
And—well the dog was game!

'He made no sign: the fires of hell were round him,
The pit of hell below.
We sat and waited, but we never found him;
And then we turned to go.

'And then—you see that rock that's grown so bristly
With chaparral and tan—
Suthin' crep' out; it might hev been a grizzly,
It might hev been a man;

'Suthin' that howled, and gnashed its teeth, and shouted
In smoke and dust and flame;
Suthin' that sprang into the depths about it,
Grizzly or man—but game!

'That's all. Well, yes, it does look rather risky,
And kinder makes one queer
And dizzy looking down. A drop of whisky
Ain't a bad thing right here!'

BRET HARTE

chaparral: dwarf oak

✄ False Dawn

My old friend, Lord O., owned a parcel of land—
A waste of wild dunes, rushes, marram and sand—
With a square Tudor mansion—not a bush, not a tree—
Looking over salt flats a full league to the sea;
    And at his demise he bequeathed it to me. . . .

It was dusk as I entered. A gull to its mates
Cackled high in the air as I passed through the gates,
And out of the distance—full twenty miles wide—
Came the resonant boom of the incoming tide:
    Gulls' scream and groundswell; and nothing beside.

In the cold of the porch I tugged at the bell,
Till the bowels of the house echoed back like a knell.
I hearkened; then peered through the hole in the lock;
And a voice, cold and clammy, inquired, 'Did you knock?'
    And there was Lord O.—in his funeral smock.

In silence he watched me, then led me upstairs
To a room where a table stood, flanked by two chairs;
For light but a dip, in an old silver stick,
With guttering grease and a long unsnuffed wick;
    And he said, 'If you're hungry, eat quick.'

So I sipped his cold water and nibbled his bread,
While he gazed softly out from the holes in his head:—
'You would hardly believe, Brown, when once I was gone,
How I craved for your company—where there is none;
    Shivered and craved—on and on.

'This house, I agree, may seem cheerless to you;
But glance from that window! By Gad, what a view!
And think, when we weary of darkness and rats,
We can share the long night with the moon and the bats,
  And wander for hours on those flats.

'And when in the East creeping daybreak shows wan,
You'll excuse me, I know, if I have to be gone.
For as soon as sounds cock-crow, the red and the grey,
It's a rule with us all—even peers must obey—
  We all have to hasten away.'

So that it is my fate now. The small hours draw near,
We shall stalk arm-in-arm in that scenery drear;
Tête-à-tête by blanched breakers discuss on and on
If it's better to be flesh and blood or mere bone,
  Till it's time for Lord O. to be gone.

Yet, doubtless he means well. I would not suggest
To shun peers with property always is best.
But insomnia, nightmare, tic-douloureux, cramp,
Have reduced me to what's little short of a scamp;
For I've hung in my hen-roost a very large lamp.
And now, well, at least four full hours before day,
Lord O., he hears cock-crow, the red and the grey
  Sighs; stares at the ocean—and hastens away.

WALTER DE LA MARE

marram: shore grass

✣ The Song-Maker

Alone in the hot sun,
On the hot sand in the sun,
Alone at the edge of the kraal,
In the dust of the dance-ground
Near the raised tobacco patch—
The women have gone to play,
And the blind Maker of Songs
Sits here, alone, all day.

The dogs sniffed him and went,
The kraal-rats peer and go,
So very still he sits
Day long, and moon to moon,
His hands slack on the sand—
And he was just the same,
This maker of tribal songs,
Before the White Men came.

His was the song that woke
The war that brought their power;
The impi went with song—
Came back with song by night.
So many years ago,
With plunder every one;
Leaving among the dead,
Ganero, his only son.

And here, all day he sits,
On the hot sand in the sun;
The children wonder if he sleeps,
And the flies think him dead,

The dogs smell him and go—
But to him is bare the lore
Of the Threshing and the Dancing Songs,
And the Chant that leads to war.

KINGSLEY FAIRBRIDGE

impi: regiment

❧ O What is that Sound?

O what is that sound which so thrills the ear
  Down in the valley drumming, drumming?
Only the scarlet soldiers, dear,
  The soldiers coming.

O what is that light I see flashing so clear
  Over the distance brightly, brightly?
Only the sun on their weapons, dear,
  As they step lightly.

O what are they doing with all that gear;
  What are they doing this morning, this morning?
Only the usual manoeuvres, dear,
  Or perhaps a warning.

O why have they left the road down there;
  Why are they suddenly wheeling, wheeling?
Perhaps a change in the orders, dear;
  Why are you kneeling?

O haven't they stopped for the doctor's care;
  Haven't they reined their horses, their horses?
Why, they are none of them wounded, dear,
  None of these forces.

O is it the parson they want with white hair;
  Is it the parson, is it, is it?
No, they are passing his gateway, dear,
  Without a visit.

O it must be the farmer who lives so near;
  It must be the farmer so cunning, so cunning?
They have passed the farm already, dear,
  And now they are running.

O where are you going? stay with me here!
   Were the vows you swore me deceiving, deceiving?
No, I promised to love you, dear,
   But I must be leaving.

O it's broken the lock and splintered the door,
   O it's the gate where they're turning, turning;
Their boots are heavy on the floor
   And their eyes are burning.

W. H. AUDEN

✣ Don't Ask for Bread

A wretched man walked up and down
To buy his dinner in the town.

At last he found a wretched place
And entered in with modest grace,

Took off his coat, took off his hat,
And wiped his feet upon the mat,

Took out his purse to count his pence
And found he had but two half-cents.

The bill of fare, he scanned it through
To see what two half-cents would do.

The only item of them all
For two half-cents was one meatball.

So to the waiter he did call
And gently whispered: One meatball.

The waiter bellowed down the hall:
This gentleman here wants one meatball.

The diners looked both one and all
To see who wanted one meatball.

The wretched man, all ill at ease
Said: A little bread, sir, if you please.

The waiter bellowed down the hall:
We don't serve bread with one meatball.

The wretched man, he felt so small,
He quickly left the dining hall.

The wretched man, he went outside
And shot himself until he died.

This is the moral of it all,
Don't ask for bread with one meatball.

ANON.

✒ Edward, Edward

'Why does your brand sae drop wi' blude,
Edward, Edward?
Why does your brand sae drop wi' blude,
And why sae sad gang ye, O?'
'O I hae kill'd my hawk sae gude,
Mither, mither;
O I hae kill'd my hawk sae gude,
And I had nae mair but he, O.'

'Your hawk's blude was never sae red,
Edward, Edward;
Your hawk's blude was never sae red,
My dear son, I tell thee, O.'
'O I hae kill'd my red-roan steed,
Mither, mither;
O I hae kill'd my red-roan steed,
That erst was sae fair and free, O.'

'Your steed was auld, and ye hae got mair,
Edward, Edward;
Your steed was auld, and ye hae got mair,
Some other dule ye dree, O.'
'O I hae kill'd my father dear,
Mither, mither;
O I hae kill'd my father dear,
Alas, and wae is me, O!'

'And whatten penance will ye dree for that,
Edward, Edward?
Whatten penance will ye dree for that?
My dear son, now tell me, O.'

'I'll set my feet in yonder boat,
Mither, mither;
I'll set my feet in yonder boat,
And I'll fare over the sea, O.'

'And what will ye do wi' your tow'rs and your ha',
Edward, Edward?
And what will ye do wi' your tow'rs and your ha',
That were sae fair to see, O?'
'I'll let them stand till they doun fa',
Mither, mither;
I'll let them stand till they doun fa',
For here never mair maun I be, O.'

'And what will you leave to your bairns and your wife,
Edward, Edward?
And what will you leave to your bairns and your wife,
When ye gang owre the sea, O?'
'The warld's room; let them beg through life;
Mither, mither;
The warld's room: let them beg through life;
For them never mair will I see, O.'

'And what will ye leave to your ain mither dear,
Edward, Edward?
And what will ye leave to your ain mither dear,
My dear son, now tell me, O?'
'The curse of hell frae me sall ye bear,
Mither, mither;
The curse of hell frae me sail ye bear;
Sic counsels ye gave to me, O!'

ANON.

dule ye dree: grief you suffer

❧ A Piazza Tragedy

The beauteous Ethel's father has a
Newly painted front piazza,
He has a
Piazza;
When with tobacco juice 'twas tainted,
They had the front piazza painted,
That tainted
Piazza painted.

Algernon called that night, perchance,
Arrayed in comely sealskin pants,
That night, perchance,
In gorgeous pants;
Engaging Ethel in a chat
On the piazza down he sat,
In chat,
They sat.

And when an hour or two had passed,
He tried to rise, but oh! stuck fast,
At last
Stuck fast!
Fair Ethel shrieked, 'It is the paint!'
And fainted in a deadly faint,
This saint
Did faint.

Algernon sits there till this day,
He cannot tear himself away;
Away?
Nay, nay,

His pants are firm, the paint is dry,
He's nothing else to do but die;
To die!
O my!

EUGENE FIELD

piazza: verandah

﷽ The Last Shift

The gate clangs and the nightshift cage descends;
And, with eyes closed against the dust and grit
That swirls up in the draught, into the pit
Once more he drops, he, with his boyhood's friends,
Old mates and cronies now this many a year,
Packed close about him; and thinking, too, maybe,
Of their sons serving in the war, as he,
Of his own lad. For, as they drop down sheer,
Down, down and down, a thousand feet or more,
Down, down and down and down into the black
And tortuous entrails of the earth, young Jack,
A pilot since the outbreak of the war,
Happen, even now, is climbing three miles high
Or thrice three miles, up, up into the rare
And icy upper reaches of the air,
Up, up and up into the brilliant night
To tackle enemy squadrons, bearing down
To pound with death some sleepy English town—
Jack, soaring through thin air in flashing flight,
As into the thick closeness of the earth
His father drops, to work nightlong and hew
The coal, Jack, fighting. . .
      Yet maybe it's true
His own work, too, is fighting; for a dearth
Of fuel for the machines, without a doubt,
Would lose the war for us. Ay, sure enough,
Even planes could never soar unless the stuff,
Metal, and coal to smelt it, were dug out
Of earth's black bowels by such men as he,
The miner-sons of miners, who know the trick
Of handling tools, cutter and wedge and pick,
Almost by instinct.
      And now suddenly
At the shaft-foot the cage stops with a jerk

Beside the lamproom, and he takes his lamp,
Burnished and newly-tested against blackdamp;
Then mounts a tub to rattle to his work
Over the jolting trolley-rails and ride
Six miles or so along a gallery,
Long stript of coal, to where, beneath the sea,
Still richly-loaded measures run—the tide
Sweeping and surging in a welter of white
Far overhead, the island-circling deep
Where restless trawlers and destroyers keep
Unwinking watch throughout the livelong night . . .
And over them, the sky where, full of pluck,
Jack fights!
     Nay, he must not let his mind run
On suchlike thoughts! Jack is their only son;
But Jack, as other men, must take his luck.
And even in the pit . . . Where should he be,
Himself, if he let his thoughts loose, sniffing all
The risks, the hundred things that might befall?
Life, at the best, was chancy: though, certainly,
War has increased the hazards: and even his wife,
Lying now snug in bed, God knows what might
Drop down on her from out of the clear night!
But he could not let his thoughts . . . And such was life
For all of us in these days; everywhere
Folk faced such hazards, knowing that each breath
Might be their last: ay, all hobnobbed with death,
Hail-fellow-well-met! by sea or land or air.

'Twas strange tonight, though, how his thoughts had
On dangers. Ay, and reaching the pithead,
He had felt like turning back again, instead
Of stepping into the cage as he had done
So often without giving it a thought,
As if he fancied he might break his neck!
And, taking his lamp and handing in his check

To the lampman, old Dick Dodd, he had even caught
Himself out, muttering 'So long!' to him,
As though he would not see his old mug again,
Or cared much if he didn't! It was plain,
Plain as Dick's mug—and that was something grim—
His wits. . . .

      His wife slept snug—Jack, overhead,
A red-haired guardian angel on the alert!
And, likely enough, neither would come to hurt
Tonight: and in the morning from her bed
His wife would rise as usual. For no wars
Could keep down Susan, always game and gay
To get things done. Even the Judgment Day
Would likely find her singing at her chores.
Ay, she would rise as usual to prepare
His breakfast and his tub and set things straight,
Against his coming. She was never late;
And he would always find things fair and square
On his return from the pit.

      And, as for Jack—
His folk had been pitfolk time out of mind;
And it took something special to down that kind
Or get them windy, even when things looked black.
Hazard was in their blood. They lived on risk,
And relished it, or took it as it came.

And now he hears somebody shout his name
Above the racket of the tubs; and brisk
And sharp he turns to answer an old jest—
He, always more than a match for anyone
When it came to ragging—while the trucks still run
Through the low dripping dusk, to come to rest,
Reaching their journey's end, with squealing brakes.
Then, nimbler yet than any, down he leaps;
And, scrambling over rocks and coaldust heaps,
And splashing through black puddles, now he takes

His way yet further along the narrow seam;
Stooping yet lower as the roof slopes down,
Rock-studded, threatening to crack his crown,
For all his leather cap; and wades a stream
That trickles from a rift in the coal-face.
Then, nigh on hands and knees, 'twixt closing walls
Into a three-foot seam he slowly crawls
And by his own coalcutter takes his place.

Crouched all night long, he works with aching bones,
Half-blind with dust and sweat: while all around
He hears the pit 'talk' as the stresses shift
And cutters grinding with harsh rasping sound,
While now and then a rattle of falling stones
Strikes sharply in his ear. Throughout the night
His thoughts are with his folk—his wife, asleep,
He trusts, in well-earned slumber, snug and deep;
And Jack above the clouds in reckless flight.
All night he works till, as the shift at last
Draws to an end, the cutter jams; and now,
Stopping to wipe a trickle from his brow,
He hears a long low rumble down the drift
That thunders nearer and nearer . . . Roofs and walls
Heave all about him, cracking . . . Blast on blast
Shatters his world for him . . . till gradually
A dreadful quiet settles; and, by falls
Of rock cut off from life, he finds himself,
Together with his old mates, Bill and Joe,
Half-stifled, blind and dazed, as they crouch low,
Huddled in darkness on a narrow shelf.

Speechless, they crouch through an eternity;
Then, chuckling brokenly, he mutters, 'Come, Bill,
Let's clear our throats and turn a tune, until
They find us—and you, Joe! What shall it be?

Come, lads, pipe up! And, happen, they may hear,
And reach us easier.' Huskily, 'The Keel Row'
He starts; then, shyly joined by Bill and Joe,
His voice through the hot dark rings true and clear.

W. W. GIBSON

✸ Casualty

They trundled him in at three o'clock, still dead
Of night, upon a trolley and left him
Swaddled in blankets while they warmed the bed.

He watched in dumb patience, his stiff limbs could not stir,
He would remember no word that was said,
But lay half smiling, drained of thought and care.

Orderlies brought white towels and cotton wool,
A screen was wheeled about him, next a chair
On which a beaker and a vomit bowl.

Such simple decor lends a kind of grace;
He felt himself soothed and handled like a fool,
Soft hands drew gentle flannels across his face.

But existence beyond lay guarded by swing doors;
Throughout the night he heard the doctors pace,
Slowly, the silent, whitewashed corridors.

Illness annuls rights, sterilizes force;
Like children expecting service for each whim
Each tries to sleep off what the blunt senses dread,
A visit to the theatre. But knives rehearse
Their dialogue with the flesh, shouts rend the dream.

Complaining of the endless pain in his head,
The patient was told that fever must run its course:
The sister went quietly out, the ward grew dim.

CHRISTOPHER LEVENSON

❧ The Lonely Farmer

Poor hill farmer astray in the grass;
There came a movement and he looked up, but
All that he saw was the wind pass.
There was a sound of voices on the air,
But where, where? It was only the glib stream talking
Softly to itself. And once when he was walking
Along a lane in spring he was deceived
By a shrill whistle coming through the leaves:
Wait a minute, wait a minute—four swift notes;
He turned, and it was nothing, only a thrush
In the thorn bushes easing its throat.
He swore at himself for paying heed,
The poor hill farmer, so often again
Stopping, staring, listening, in vain,
His ear betrayed by the heart's need.

R. S. THOMAS

❧ The Stone

And will you cut a stone for him,
To set above his head?
And will you cut a stone for him—
A stone for him? she said.

Three days before a splintered rock
Had struck her lover dead—
Had struck him in the quarry dead,
Where, careless of the warning call,
He loitered while the shot was fired—
A lively stripling, brave and tall,
And sure of all his heart desired . . .
A flash, a shock,
A rumbling fall . . .
And broken 'neath the broken rock,
A lifeless heap with face of clay,
And still as any stone, he lay
With eyes that saw the end of all.

I went to break the news to her,
And I could hear my own heart beat
With dread of what my lips might say;
But some poor fool had sped before
And flinging wide her father's door,
Had blurted out the news to her,
Had struck her lover dead for her,
Had struck the girl's heart dead in her,
Had struck life lifeless at a word
And dropped it at her feet,
Then hurried on his witless way,
Scarce knowing she had heard.
And when I came she stood alone—
A woman turned to stone,
And though no word at all she said,
I knew that all was known.

Because her heart was dead
She did not sigh nor moan.
His mother wept:
She could not weep.
Her lover slept:
She could not sleep.
Three days, three nights,
She did not stir;
Three days, three nights,
Were one to her,
Who never closed her eyes
From sunset to sunrise,
From dawn to evenfall,
Her tearless staring eyes
That, seeing naught, saw all.

The fourth night when I came from work
I found her at my door.
And will you cut a stone for him?
She said, and spoke no more,
But followed me as I went in,
And sank upon a chair,
And fixed her grey eyes on my face
With still unseeing stare.
And as she waited patiently
I could not bear to feel
Those still grey eyes that followed me,
Those eyes that plucked the heart from me,
Those eyes that sucked the breath from me,
And curdled the warm blood in me,
Those eyes that cut me to the bone
And pierced my marrow like cold steel.

And so I rose and sought a stone,
And cut it smooth and square;
And as I worked she sat and watched

Beside me in her chair.
Night after night by candlelight
I cut her lover's name;
Night after night so still and white
And like a ghost she came,
And sat beside me in her chair
And watched with eyes aflame.

She eyed each stroke,
And hardly stirred:
She never spoke
A single word:
And not a sound or murmur broke
The quiet save the mallet-stroke.
With still eyes ever on my hands,
With eyes that seemed to burn my hands,
My wincing over-wearied hands,
She watched with bloodless lips apart
And silent indrawn breath;
And every stroke my chisel cut,
Death cut still deeper in her heart—
The two of us were chiselling
Together, I and death.

And when at length the job was done
And I had laid the mallet by,
As if at last her peace were won
She breathed his name, and with a sigh
Passed slowly through the open door,
And never crossed my threshold more.

Next night I laboured late, alone,
To cut her name too on the stone.

W. W. GIBSON

✺ The Swans

Midstream they met. Challenger and champion,
They fought a war for honour
Fierce, sharp, but with no honour:
Each had a simple aim and sought it quickly.
The combat over, the victor sailed away
Broken, but placid as is the gift of swans,
Leaving his rival to his shame alone.
I listened for a song, according to story,
But this swan's death was out of character—
No giving up of the grace of life
In a sad lingering music.
I saw the beaten swan rise on the water
As though to outreach pain, its webbed feet
Banging the river helplessly, its wings
Loose in a last hysteria. Then the neck
Was floating like a rope and the swan was dead.
It drifted away and all around it swan's-down
Bobbed on the river like children's little boats.

CLIFFORD DYMENT

The 'story' referred to in l. 8 is the ancient fable that the swan
(which does not sing in the sense that we normally understand
birdsong) sings beautifully just before death.

✍ Out, Out—

The buzz-saw snarled and rattled in the yard
And made dust and dropped stove-length sticks of wood,
Sweet-scented stuff when the breeze drew across it.
And from there those that lifted eyes could count
Five mountain ranges one behind the other
Under the sunset far into Vermont.
And the saw snarled and rattled, snarled and rattled,
As it ran light, or had to bear a load.
And nothing happened; day was all but done.
Call it a day, I wish they might have said
To please the boy by giving him the half hour
That a boy counts so much when saved from work.
His sister stood beside them in her apron
To tell them 'Supper'. At the word, the saw,
As if to prove saws knew what supper meant,
Leaped out at the boy's hand, or seemed to leap—
He must have given the hand. However, it was,
Neither refused the meeting. But the hand!
The boy's first outcry was a rueful laugh,
As he swung toward them holding up the hand
Half in appeal, but half as if to keep
The life from spilling. Then the boy saw all—
Since he was old enough to know, big boy
Doing a man's work, though a child at heart—
He saw all spoiled. 'Don't let him cut my hand off—
The doctor, when he comes. Don't let him, sister!'
So. But the hand was gone already.
The doctor put him in the dark of ether.
He lay and puffed his lips out with his breath.
And then—the watcher at his pulse took fright.

No one believed. They listened at his heart.
Little—less—nothing! and that ended it.
No more to build on there. And they, since they
Were not the one dead, turned to their affairs.

ROBERT FROST

❧ The Survivors

I never told you this.
He told me about it often:
Seven days in an open boat—burned out,
No time to get food:
Biscuits and water and the unwanted sun,
With only the oars' wing-beats for motion,
Labouring heavily towards land
That existed on a remembered chart,
Never on the horizon
Seven miles from the boat's bow.

After two days song dried on their lips;
After four days speech.
On the fifth cracks began to appear
In the faces' masks; salt scorched them.
They began to think about death,
Each man to himself, feeding it
On what the rest could not conceal.
The sea was as empty as the sky,
A vast disc under a dome
Of the same vastness, perilously blue.

But on the sixth day towards evening
A bird passed. No one slept that night;
The boat had become an ear
Straining for the desired thunder
Of the wrecked waves. It was dawn when it came,
Ominous as the big guns
Of enemy shores. The men cheered it.
From the swell's rise one of them saw the ruins
Of all that sea, where a lean horseman
Rode towards them and with a rope
Galloped them up on to the curt sand.

R. S. THOMAS

❧ Saturday Storm

This flooded morning is no time to be
Abroad on any business of mankind.
The rain has lost its casual charity;
It falls and falls and falls and would not mind
Were all the world washed blind.

No creature out of doors goes weatherproof.
Birds cower in their nests. The beast that can
Has found himself a roof.
This hour's for man
To waken late in, putter by his fire,
Leaf through old books or tear old letters up,
Mend household things with bits of thrifty wire,
Refill his coffee cup,
And, thus enclosed in comfort like a shell,
Give thought to, wish them well
Who must this day
On customary errands take their way:

The glistening policemen in the street,
For instance, blowing their whistles through the welter
And stamping their wet feet;
And grocery boys flung in and out of shelter
But faithful to their loads;
And people changing tyres beside the roads;
Doormen with colds and doctors in damp suits;
And milkmen on their routes,
Scuttling like squirrels; and men with cleated boots
Aloft on telephone poles in the rough gale;
But chiefly trudging men with sacks of mail
Slung over shoulder,
Who slog from door to door and cannot rest
Till they've delivered the last government folder,
The final scribbled postcard, misaddressed.

Oh, all at ease
Should say a prayer for these—
That they come, healthy, homeward before night,
Safer than beasts or birds,
To no dark welcome but an earned delight
Of pleasant words,
Known walls, accustomed love, fires burning steady,
And a good dinner ready.

PHYLLIS MCGINLEY

❧ I was a Labourer in the Smoky Valley

I was a labourer in the smoky valley,
within the high wall, the tall dark walls of the mills,
where the hills go up to the wild moor.
I am a dog of the dales, broad is my speech,
and my ways are not the smooth ways of the south,
but hard, and used to keener weather.
All week I worked among the looms
while the cloth slacked out and the shuttles clacked
swiftly, as the woof was shot through the warp
and through my brain dim with the webs of years.
All week I was the servant of the loom,
chained to the steel for the promise of meagre coin,
six days a week, but Sunday comes
soon, and I am my master for the waking day
that found me with my whippet on the moor.
O my faithful lass! Soft was her fell;
her eyes were like deep pools stained with peat,
shafted with light; and intelligent.
She was long in the body, but strong of limb and rib,
and her muscles moved under the skin
like currents in a bay of the river.
She was swift as the wind or as the summer swallow,
and I would pit her with the local dogs,
backing her swiftness with my sweaty coin
and many a shilling have I won with her
to spend on some wet evening in a pub
or buy the tickets at the picture palace
when I took out the girl I meant to marry—
but that is all forgotten with the flesh.
I was a labourer in the smoky valley:
I am a brittle bone projecting from the sand.

SEAN JENNETT   *fell*: skin

❧ Winter Warfare

Colonel Cold strode up the Line
(tabs of rime and spurs of ice);
stiffened all that met his glare:
horses, men and lice.

Visited a forward post,
left them burning, ear to foot;
fingers stuck to biting steel,
toes to frozen boot.

Stalked on into No Man's Land,
turned the wire to fleecy wool,
iron stakes to sugar sticks
snapping at a pull.

Those who watched with hoary eyes
saw two figures gleaming there;
Hauptmann Kalte, Colonel Cold,
gaunt in the grey air.

Stiffly, tinkling spurs they moved,
glassy eyed, with glinting heel,
Stabbing those who lingered there
torn by screaming steel.

EDGELL RICKWORD

Then Jesus went with His disciples into the villages round Caesarea Philippi; and on the way He asked His disciples, 'Who do men say that I am?' They answered, 'John the Baptist, and others say Elias; others that Thou art like one of the prophets.' Then He said to them, 'And what of you? Who do you say that I am?' Peter answered Him, 'Thou art the Christ.' (Mark 8.)

And Jesus answered Him, 'Blessed art thou, Simon son of Jona; it is not flesh and blood, it is My Father in heaven that has revealed this to thee. And I tell thee this in my turn, that thou art Peter, and it is upon this rock that I will build My church; and the gates of hell shall not prevail against it.' (Matthew 16.)

ஜ Peter

For a while, Mark, lay your scroll aside.
I need your eyes. When I'm dictating
I think in words. That kind of thinking
Blurs what's behind the words. You see,
I'm no scholar, friend—nor ever will be.
Words come hardly to me, very hardly.
Though I have fought them for our Master's sake,
I'll never be their master. Talking's all right:
You see the other's face; talking is natural.
But when I watch you setting down my speech
In black and white, it puts my tongue in fetters.
So this evening, Mark, just let me say
My memories to you. I want to recall
This clearer than the rest—it most concerns me.

I would remember and re-live
What happened on the road to Caesarea,
Those years ago.
We were walking despondently towards the city
Discouraged and alone. Driven from Galilee,
Each had his own regrets. Yes, even He
Was sorrowful—I sensed it—saying little,
Scarcely answering . . . Then all at once
The sound of water. We raised our heads,
And, rearing over us, a cliff of limestone,
Brilliant in sunlight. Streaks of iron, like blood,
Ran down it, and from a cave
Half down the rock, the Jordan river
Descending from the heights of Hermon,
Poured out its spring-clear waters. We stopped,
Seeing the city of Caesarea
Behind a lace of spray—the trees,
White roofs and towers. It should have lifted us,
That sudden vision. Somehow it didn't.
It made us more despondent. For I thought—
Or was it He who thought and I who felt Him?—
This water that is born so hopefully
Ends in the Dead Sea's useless desolation.
Abruptly He asked, 'Who do men say I am?'
We answered variously, 'John the Baptist, risen,'
'Elijah or Jeremiah,' 'One of the prophets.'
Silence, the water speaking. Then He asked:
'Who do *you* say I am?' Another silence—
Only a moment, but enough to tell
Our disillusionment. I cried—
No, rather I heard the words drawn from me—
The voice was not my own: 'You are the Christ,
Son of the Living God!' He turned to me
Transfigured. His face was God's.

'Peter' (He named me then), 'You are the rock
On which I build my church. The gates of hell
Shall not prevail against you.' Oh, Mark,
Men have their moments.—That was mine,
The phrase I'd lived for. Since then
I have betrayed it—doubted, denied,
Deserted Him. But always
Those words return, with their background
Of falling water, each time
More powerful than before. For He saw me,
Not as I was, but as I might become.
His faith has hardened me. In course of time
The rock has petrified. When that hour comes
When I must follow Him who questioned me,
I shall not fail again. The gates of hell,
As He once prophesied, shall not prevail.'

CLIVE SANSOM

INDEX OF FIRST LINES

159